TWELVE ANGRY MEN

THE GREENHAVEN PRESS
Literary Companion
TO AMERICAN LITERATURE

READINGS ON

TWELVE ANGRY MEN

Russ Munyan, *Book Editor*

David L. Bender, *Publisher*
Bruno Leone, *Executive Editor*
Bonnie Szumski, *Series Editor*

Greenhaven Press, Inc., San Diego, CA

Every effort has been made to trace the owners of copyrighted material. The articles in this volume may have been edited for content, length, and/or reading level. The titles have been changed to enhance the editorial purpose. Those interested in locating the original source will find the complete citation on the first page of each article.

Library of Congress Cataloging-in-Publication Data

Readings on Twelve angry men / Russ Munyan, book editor.
        p.   cm. — (The Greenhaven Press literary
    companion to American literature)
    Includes bibliographical references and index.
    ISBN 0-7377-0314-8 (lib. bdg. : alk. paper). —
ISBN 0-7377-0313-X (pbk. : alk. paper)
    1. Rose, Reginald. Twelve angry men. 2. Rose,
Reginald—Film and video adaptations. 3. Trials in
motion pictures. 4. Trials in literature. 5. Jury in motion
pictures. 6. Jury in literature. 7. 12 angry men. I. Title:
Twelve angry men. II. Munyan, Russ. III. Series.
PS3535.O666 T937   2000
812'.54—dc21
                                                        99-055869
                                                             CIP

Cover photo: Archive Photos

Copyright ©2000 by Greenhaven Press, Inc.
PO Box 289009
San Diego, CA 92198-9009
Printed in the U.S.A.

"Twelve Angry Men *is, at base, not about guilt and innocence but about democracy. And it moves us most deeply when it shows us that men—not least these jurymen—should be allowed to have their own lifestyles and opinions without being bullied or persecuted for having them.*"

—Alastair Macaulay

CONTENTS

Chapter 1: Insights from the Makers of *Twelve Angry Men*

of filming, editing, and distributing the film, all of which made him want to never produce a film again.

Chapter 2: Scholarly Analysis of *Twelve Angry Men*

Chapter 3: Critical Reviews of *Twelve Angry Men*

FOREWORD

*"'Tis the good reader that
makes the good book."*

Ralph Waldo Emerson

The story's bare facts are simple: The captain, an old and scarred seafarer, walks with a peg leg made of whale ivory. He relentlessly drives his crew to hunt the world's oceans for the great white whale that crippled him. After a long search, the ship encounters the whale and a fierce battle ensues. Finally the captain drives his harpoon into the whale, but the harpoon line catches the captain about the neck and drags him to his death.

A simple story, a straightforward plot—yet, since the 1851 publication of Herman Melville's *Moby-Dick*, readers and critics have found many meanings in the struggle between Captain Ahab and the whale. To some, the novel is a cautionary tale that depicts how Ahab's obsession with revenge leads to his insanity and death. Others believe that the whale represents the unknowable secrets of the universe and that Ahab is a tragic hero who dares to challenge fate by attempting to discover this knowledge. Perhaps Melville intended Ahab as a criticism of Americans' tendency to become involved in well-intentioned but irrational causes. Or did Melville model Ahab after himself, letting his fictional character express his anger at what he perceived as a cruel and distant god?

Although literary critics disagree over the meaning of *Moby-Dick*, readers do not need to choose one particular interpretation in order to gain an understanding of Melville's novel. Instead, by examining various analyses, they can gain numerous insights into the issues that lie under the surface of the basic plot. Studying the writings of literary critics can also aid readers in making their own assessments of *Moby-Dick* and other literary works and in developing analytical thinking skills.

The Greenhaven Literary Companion Series was created with these goals in mind. Designed for young adults, this unique anthology series provides an engaging and comprehensive introduction to literary analysis and criticism. The essays included in the Literary Companion Series are chosen for their accessibility to a young adult audience and are expertly edited in consideration of both the reading and comprehension levels of this audience. In addition, each essay is introduced by a concise summation that presents the contributing writer's main themes and insights. Every anthology in the Literary Companion Series contains a varied selection of critical essays that cover a wide time span and express diverse views. Wherever possible, primary sources are represented through excerpts from authors' notebooks, letters, and journals and through contemporary criticism.

Each title in the Literary Companion Series pays careful consideration to the historical context of the particular author or literary work. In-depth biographies and detailed chronologies reveal important aspects of authors' lives and emphasize the historical events and social milieu that influenced their writings. To facilitate further research, every anthology includes primary and secondary source bibliographies of articles and/or books selected for their suitability for young adults. These engaging features make the Greenhaven Literary Companion Series ideal for introducing students to literary analysis in the classroom or as a library resource for young adults researching the world's great authors and literature.

Exceptional in its focus on young adults, the Greenhaven Literary Companion Series strives to present literary criticism in a compelling and accessible format. Every title in the series is intended to spark readers' interest in leading American and world authors, to help them broaden their understanding of literature, and to encourage them to formulate their own analyses of the literary works that they read. It is the editors' hope that young adult readers will find these anthologies to be true companions in their study of literature.

INTRODUCTION

To those with a basic knowledge of classic American films, *Twelve Angry Men* is a familiar title. The great American film actor Henry Fonda, who both starred in and co-produced the film, considered it one of the important films of his career.

Yet *Twelve Angry Men* did not start as a film. It was first performed as a 1954 live television drama, which is a format and time long past. Live television drama has simply not been regularly performed in nearly two generations. Nevertheless, live TV is the unusual source for this often studied film piece.

That uncommon source makes *Twelve Angry Men* an uncommon, albeit valuable, object of academic study. It is regularly taught at the secondary and college level in a variety of disciplines, including literature, communication, sociology, and history. Yet relatively few scholarly essays and articles have been written about *Twelve Angry Men*, as much of its commentary has been in the form of brief film reviews. But a number of the scholarly essays that have been written on the piece are included in this collection.

There have been four major versions of "Twelve Angry Men,"[1] written by playwright Reginald Rose (1920–). First was the 1954 teleplay. When it aired, it was about fifty minutes long, but it had been written with an additional twenty minutes of dialogue that had to be cut for the sake of time.

The second version of *Twelve Angry Men* was the ninety-five minute 1957 Henry Fonda film. Rose wrote the third version in 1960 as a live theater play, which has been in virtual

---

1. Since the TV version of "Twelve Angry Men" was a single episode of a weekly television anthology (*Studio One*), its title is written non-italicized and with quotation marks. The other three versions of *Twelve Angry Men* are all full-length, stand-alone pieces; their titles are written italicized and without quotation marks. Further, some of the authors in this collection write the title as *Twelve Angry Men*, while others write it as *12 Angry Men*. But since playwright Reginald Rose's own printing of the play in his book *Six Television Plays* (1956) uses the alphabetic instead of the numeric form, that is what the editorial additions in this collection use.

constant performance on both the professional and amateur stage ever since. The fourth version was a full-length made-for-television movie by the cable channel Showtime in 1997. It was just under two hours long, and boasted an all-star cast led by Jack Lemmon, George C. Scott, and Hume Cronyn.

This collection of essays about *Twelve Angry Men* is the only anthology of its kind. Some of the articles included within are currently used in some classrooms, but virtually none of the instructors asked who have written about or are using *Twelve Angry Men* is familiar with more than one—or at most a few—of these documents. This collection brings together several of the major writings about the play for the first time in order to further its utility as an educational tool.

REGINALD ROSE: A BIOGRAPHY

When "Twelve Angry Men" was first performed as a live television broadcast in 1954, probably no one expected that the story would endure beyond its original airing. After all, in those days there was no way of making broadcast-quality video recordings of television productions (thus TV shows were broadcast live), so that "Twelve Angry Men" could be re-broadcast. And even with the low-quality video recording technology that did exist—called kinescopes—only the second half of the original broadcast was ever saved. Furthermore, the sheer number of live television dramas at that time—343 in the 1954–1955 season alone—worked against "Twelve Angry Men" ever becoming permanently memorable.

The playwright himself, Reginald Rose, did not appear to be on a mission to create an undying work. While he no doubt took pride in his work, he seemed to be writing with fairly mundane objectives. Consider this excerpt from his 1956 book, *Six Television Plays*, which includes the "Twelve Angry Men" script.

> Should anyone be interested in the history of [my] relatively brief career in television and how it came about, I submit the following. My first television play, which was performed in December 1951, was a half-hour original, written in sheer desperation as a protest against the nightly agonies television had to offer. Those of you who had television sets in 1951 will know what I mean. As I look at it now, what I had written merely added more agony to the pile. But it did pay me $650, and open my eyes to a brand-new method for keeping the pot boiling (the only problem at the time being the ability to afford a pot). That play shall remain nameless, as shall the next dozen plays I turned out, all of which were written between January 1952 and November 1953, and all of which were uniformly mediocre. During this period I worked as a copywriter for a small advertising agency specializing in men's and women's wear, and all of my television writing was done at night and on week ends. I realized that these sixteen-hour days were becoming ridiculous when I found myself referring to my oldest boy, then four years of age, as "what's-his-name."

(The happy solution to this dilemma should appear here, I believe. I now work a four-hour day and know all four boys' names at all times.)

Finally, in November of 1953, with considerable urging on the part of Florence Britton, [TV anthology] *Studio One*'s story editor, I wrote my first hour-long original drama, "The Remarkable Incident at Carson Corners." Not long after that the advertising business and I parted ways, both of us immeasurably brightened, and both probably the richer for it. Since then I have written some fourteen one-hour original plays for television. . . . I have enjoyed myself thoroughly, spent a great deal of leisure time with my wife and family, and managed to pay most of the bills by the tenth of the month.

This kind of creative and financial fulfillment was beyond my reach before I began writing for television, although I had earned my living as a writer for five years previous to my television debut. As an advertising copywriter I must admit that the work I did was creative, though a bit stifling perhaps. Sample: "This lovely wisp of a girdle effortlessly tucks you in at the tummy, as it flattens you at the derriere!" For five years I had wanted to call a spade a spade, and a derriere a behind. Television finally allowed me this pleasure. . . . For an ex-advertising writer this was the rarest of ambrosia. End of history.[1]

Yet despite Rose's levity in 1956, twenty-six years later he would say of the 1950s and 1960s, "So many of the things I wrote about in those days were burning issues. Injustices and outrages that I saw bothered me. I saw them and I wanted to fight against them."[2]

Perhaps that passion gave "Twelve Angry Men" the life it needed to prevent it from disappearing into oblivion, as nearly all of the 1950s live dramas did. It certainly caught the nation's attention that night it first aired in 1954. A *Variety* magazine TV critic wrote, "The play was a whammo."[3]

Following its 1954 fifty-minute television showing, actor Henry Fonda approached Rose about making "Twelve Angry Men" into a full-length feature movie. The two of them decided to coproduce the film. Rose had "cut large chunks of dialogue"[4] from his original script in order to fit it into the length of a telecast, so the film allowed him to restore those portions, most of which involved character development. Fonda and Rose raised the $340,000 for the cost of the production themselves.

The film was released in 1957 as a conventional booking in large theaters, but it was a commercial failure. Fonda had wanted to distribute the film only to small art theaters, where it might have gained a major following and run for months on the strength of the reviews that he believed it would (and did) get; later, hindsight proved that this would have been the smarter choice. However, the investors had disagreed, so Fonda and Rose had no choice, and into the larger theaters it went. Though the film was a critical success, it failed to make a profit, and Fonda never received his deferred salary. Despite his financial loss, Fonda remembered it fondly as one of his three best efforts (along with *The Grapes of Wrath* and *The Ox-Bow Incident*). Today it is generally considered not only one of the great films of the 1950s, but a classic American film.

Whatever the reason that *Twelve Angry Men* has become a lasting fixture of Americana, the work remains a part of the nation's culture, as evidenced by cable television channel Showtime's 1997 remake of the 1957 film, this time featuring an all-star cast led by two-time Oscar winner Jack Lemmon. As *Newsday* wrote in its review of that remake, "It's as germane today as in 1954, 1957 or 1960, when Rose reworked it into a play that's been staged virtually nonstop around the globe ever since."[5]

Playwright Reginald Rose

Reginald Rose was born in New York City in 1920, the son of William (a lawyer) and Alice (Obendorfer) Rose. He attended (but did not graduate from) City College, now of the City University of New York (CUNY).

In his young adulthood he held a variety of jobs, including working as a camp counselor and as different types of clerks: file, receiving, and stock. In 1943 he married Barbara Langbart, and four sons were born of that marriage: Jonathan, Richard, and Andrew and Steven (twins). During World War II he served in the Army Quartermaster Corps (from 1942 to 1946) as an enlisted man and then as an officer, completing his service as a first lieutenant. After the war he returned to New York, where he worked as a publicist for Warner Brothers Pictures and as an account executive and copy chief for a small advertising agency.

He sold his first teleplay, "The Bus to Nowhere," a half-hour live drama, to CBS in 1951. It aired in December of that year on the show *Out There*. He recalled in 1986, "I had been trying to sell short stories, novels, and God knows what else and I was never able to sell anything. The first time I wrote a TV script I sold it and when I had sold that first one they said, 'More, More, More!' and I haven't stopped since."[6] That success led to his writing numerous television scripts in the 1950s and '60s.

STUDIO ONE

In November 1953, Rose completed his first hour-long original drama. It was for CBS's *Studio One*, a weekly anthology of live television drama for which he would become a regular writer. The play was "The Remarkable Incident at Carson Corners," in which a group of schoolchildren try their school's janitor for murder for pushing a child off the fire escape. Over the course of the trial, the audience learns that the fire escape was faulty because the community did not want to pay to fix up the old school. The public response was strong, and kinescopes of the show were shown for years thereafter to schools and civic groups.

About that time, Rose read a news story about white residents of Cicero, Illinois, who had reacted negatively when they learned that some African Americans would be moving into the community. Rose was appalled. "The inhuman, medieval attitudes of those free, white Americans had so disturbed me that I decided to do a play about them in an attempt to expose the causes behind their mass sickness."[7] His idea for "Thunder on Sycamore Street" was to tell the story by focusing each act on a different house on the block during the same period of time. The first act is set in the home of Frank and his wife, Clarice, a racist couple discussing whether the other white neighbors shared their anger at the coming desegregation of their community. The second act portrays Arthur and his wife, Phyllis, who are not as sure as Frank that action should be taken against the newcomers. The final act introduces Joe Blake, the object of the neighborhood action, as he faces up to a crowd of his new neighbors.

By the time Rose completed the script, it was 1954, the same year that the *Brown v. Board of Education* decision outlawed segregated schools. The problem with the play's idea, Rose said later, was that "Everybody knew [you could not do a story about blacks moving into a white neighborhood], except me. Oh, I knew, but I thought I could maybe get it by." Florence Britton, *Studio One*'s story editor, took him to lunch and explained the facts of network life: The hero of such a story could not be black because the South would object. Rose "felt that a compromise would weaken the play but I decided to make one anyway, hoping that the principle under observation was strong enough to rouse an audience."[8]

The character of Blake was changed to a white ex-convict, but as Rose rewrote the play, he only revealed this to the audience in the middle of act 2, so before this they could only imagine what Blake's "sin" might have been. Audiences responded as Rose had anticipated. In the mail that poured in after the show's broadcast on March 15, 1954, viewers reasoned that the ex-con was a symbol, but interpretations varied. Differing viewers thought Joe Blake stood for a black, a Puerto Rican, a Japanese, a Chinese, a Russian, an ex-Communist, an anarchist, a Jew, a Catholic, or an avowed atheist. Rose wrote, "Not one person I spoke to felt that he was actually meant to be an ex-convict, and perhaps 'Thunder on Sycamore Street' had more value in its various interpretations than it would have had it simply presented the Negro problem."[9] A week after the show, Rose got a letter from ten married couples in the West saying that events like that could never happen in America.

Rose's work for *Studio One* (1948–1958) vaulted him to national prominence as a television writer, and it was at *Studio One* that "Twelve Angry Men" premiered in 1954. Following his work on *Studio One*, Rose created and supervised the successful television series *The Defenders* (1961–1965), an early show about trial lawyers and the law profession; he also wrote many of its episodes. For his work on *The Defenders*, he won Emmy Awards in 1962 and 1963 and a Writer's Guild of America Award in 1962.

By this time, Rose and his first wife had divorced, and in 1963 he married Ellen McLaughlin. Of that union two additional sons were born, Thomas and Christopher.

Rose has continued to write for television in every decade from the 1960s through the 1990s. His later works include the *Studs Lonigan* miniseries in 1979, *Escape from Sobibor* in 1987 (for which he received a Writer's Guild of America Laurel Award), and TV movie remakes of *Twelve Angry Men* and *The Defenders* in the 1990s. In addition to receiving three Emmy Awards, he has been nominated for three others.

Beyond his television writing, Rose has written five plays for the live stage, including *Black Monday* in 1962 and *This Agony, This Triumph* in 1972, as well as live-action rewrites of *Twelve Angry Men* in 1960, 1964, and 1996. In addition to the 1957 film version of *Twelve Angry Men*, he has written eleven screenplays from 1956 to 1985, including *The Wild Geese* (1978) and *Whose Life Is It, Anyway?* (1981, cowritten with Brian Clark). The film *Twelve Angry Men* received three Academy Award nominations, for Best Picture, Best Director, and Best Screenplay for Material Based on Another Medium. It won the Edgar Allan Poe Award for Best Motion Picture Screenplay and the Berlin Film Festival Golden Bear Award (first place). Rose has also published two books: *Six Television Plays* (1956), which includes six of Rose's scripts along with his commentary, and *The Thomas Book* (1972), dedicated to his son Thomas, which is a short children's book set in Africa about a boy named Thomas and his large family.

THE GENESIS OF "TWELVE ANGRY MEN"

The genesis of "Twelve Angry Men" was in Rose's own experience as a juror on a manslaughter case in New York City. When he was first summoned to be a juror, he had what could be considered a fairly common reaction: "grumblings and mutterings." But, he writes, his entire attitude changed the moment he entered the courtroom and found himself "facing a strange man whose fate was more or less in my hands." He continues, "This was my first experience on a jury and it left quite an impression on me. . . . I doubt whether I have ever been so impressed in my life with a role I had to play, and I suddenly became so earnest that, in thinking about it later, I was probably unbearable to the eleven other jurors." It occurred to him then "that a play taking place entirely within a jury room might be an exciting and possibly moving experience for an audience."[10] The audience that Rose had in mind was the 1950s American television audience.

1950s TELEVISION

In the 1950s, television was a relatively new form of technology. Radio had been the dominant mass communication technology in the decades prior. The first regular television broadcasts began in 1939, but after two years they were suspended until shortly after World War II in 1945. A television broadcast boom began in 1946, and the industry then grew rapidly, with 55 percent of American households having one or more TV sets by 1953 and 67 percent of households having at least one by 1955.

One promise of the early years of TV broadcasting was

that television would provide a theater in every home. In the first half of the 1950s, that promise was made good through several weekly anthologies that broadcast live television dramas, such as *The Kraft Television Theater, Robert Montgomery Presents, The Philco TV Playhouse, The Goodyear Television Playhouse,* and *Studio One,* which aired "Twelve Angry Men" on September 20, 1954. These shows were all presented live, and they had only limited similarities from week to week, such as a master of ceremonies, theme music, and a sponsor spokesperson. The remainder of each show was an original live drama, with plots and characters typically unrelated to previous or future episodes.

Because of the heavy reliance on live original theater, this period became known as the Golden Age of Television. But despite the nostalgia associated with those times, they were not necessarily easy or flawless. Television at that time was a new medium with few established rules, making it an exciting and creative time. Many of its young directors, such as Sidney Lumet, Yul Brenner, and John Frankenheimer, had experience in live theater. Unlike film directors, who enjoyed the luxury of multiple takes with extensive editing and large budgets, the early TV directors had to handle typically inexperienced actors performing in live shows that were staged with absolute time limits. In 1997, Rose recalled working in the Golden Age:

> It was a terrifying experience, but very exhilarating. But there were always mistakes. Things always went wrong. I don't recall a show I ever did when something didn't go wrong. A show would come in short. It would come in long. A camera might start to [break down], and they had to figure out at that moment how to do it with two cameras, but these things were always solved somehow. . . . Even on "Twelve Angry Men," there were flubs all the way through. The scene was one jury room with three walls and three cameras trying to negotiate around. At least three times during the show one camera caught another camera backing out or backing in. I remember that sometimes the actors went up and forgot lines and had to ad-lib. By the time I did *The Defenders,* we were on film, and there is nothing more boring than being on a film set, reshooting and relighting and so on. There is more comfort, certainly, but not as much satisfaction. Live television—those were the tensest times I can remember, but when it was over, you really thought you had accomplished something.[11]

For writers, television was a giant opportunity. As Rose explained, "It was the only medium I've ever encountered where you could earn a living by working on scripts and at the same time learn how to write. . . . I was being handed script-writing jobs over at CBS, on *Studio One*, while I still held on to a daytime job writing copy at an advertising agency. Eventually I had made enough of an impact to give up my day job and go into writing full-time—but in the meantime, I'd been gifted with a chance to learn my craft."[12]

The live television dramas continued into the early 1960s, but they quickly died out after that. The main reason was that improving budgets and technology allowed for more filmed productions, which were, of course, of consistently better quality, since any mistakes were simply reshot and then edited out. But there were other reasons, too. Many filmed shows were sold in serial format, which allowed audiences to get involved with recurring characters. Series loyalty, in turn, prompted higher ratings. Live TV drama writers were simply not able to come up with plots each week that were strong enough to get audiences involved in each episode's new characters. Thus, while many series from the 1960s are still part of the public consciousness, almost all of the live dramas have long since been forgotten.

The television audiences of the 1950s were used to live dramas throughout the week. But those dramas were not the only things that were on TV at that time. Throughout the 1940s, Americans had spent many hours watching news reports and live coverage of the U.S. House of Representatives Un-American Activities Committee, and they provided fertile ground for the 1950s televised Senate investigations led by and subsequently of Senator Joseph R. McCarthy. These hearings in both decades had a significant effect on the American culture, especially the entertainment industry, of which Reginald Rose was a part.

THE HUAC INVESTIGATIONS

Throughout the 1940s, many conservatives in the American political arena became fearful of significant advances in global communism, specifically Soviet leader Joseph Stalin's imperialist postures and the rise of Red China under Mao Tse-tung. Yet, in many liberal circles, Communist ideas had been fashionable in between the two World Wars and shortly after World War II. It is estimated that from the middle 1930s to the middle 1950s, as many as three hundred Hollywood actors, writers, and directors joined the Communist Party. The former secretary of the Southern California Communist Party estimated that membership in the party reached a wartime high of four thousand. But given the advances and atrocities of these Communist regimes overseas, with their demonstrated imperialistic tendencies, and the accompanying birth of the cold war, conservative American elements came to treat Western Communists and Communist sympathizers as enemies of society and the American way of life. These anti-Communist concerns were acted upon with vigor in the late 1940s by the House Un-American Activities Committee (HUAC).

The HUAC began to investigate suspected Communists and sympathizers from multiple facets of society, but no social element was more rigorously scrutinized than the high-profile entertainment industry. These investigations resulted in an industry blacklist that began in the fall of 1947 and continued until the 1960s. People working in film, television, radio, and theater who were suspected of having ties to the Communist Party—whether directly or by having associations with other suspected or known Communists—were blacklisted and ostracized by the industry. Hundreds were fired from their jobs and were unable to get new ones. Others were shunned and unable to get work in the industry because of their beliefs or associations. Because the blacklisting was secret, no one knows how many people were actually affected.

In October 1947, the HUAC held hearings as an "investigation of communism in motion pictures." The HUAC not only looked into the question of subversive content in movies, but also looked into the political affiliations of the people who made the movies and the entertainment industry in general. Forty-one witnesses were subpoenaed for that round of hearings. Nineteen of them protested loudly and defiantly by declaring themselves to be "unfriendly" to Congress, refusing to answer questions concerning their political beliefs or to inform on the activities and beliefs of others in the entertainment industry. Despite that they all were or had been members of the Communist Party, they refused to admit it before Congress, insisting that the committee's questions violated their constitutional rights and that they had done nothing illegal.

As the hearings got under way, the one now-famous question that the committee eventually asked each witness was "Are you now or have you ever been a member of the Communist Party of the United States?" After calling only eleven of the "unfriendly" witnesses (as well as a number of "friendly," or cooperative, witnesses), the committee suspended its hearings; then in the following month, it charged ten of the eleven with contempt of Congress for their refusal to cooperate. Committee chairman J. Parnell Thomas, a Democrat from New Jersey, warned the industry to "set about immediately to clean its own house and not wait for public opinion to do so."[13] After a long legal battle that went all the way to the Supreme Court, which declined to hear the appeals, each of the Hollywood Ten, as they came to be known, went to prison in 1950 for periods ranging from six months to a year. Each was also fined $1,000.

This resulted in a new set of HUAC hearings—or "witch-hunts" as their critics labeled them—in 1951. The only intent of these hearings was to look into the pasts of accused Communists and sympathizers (both current and former), not to look into film content. As a result of the testimony given in the hearings, more than two hundred individuals in the entertainment industry were named by the HUAC as Communists or Communist sympathizers, and countless others were judged by the industry and pressure groups as guilty by association.

At first, many in the industry reacted openly and strongly against the hearings and the resulting criminal charges and blacklisting. But early support for the Hollywood Ten waned because of their ugly combative approach to the HUAC. It also quickly became clear that anyone who opposed the process—regardless of the reason for that opposition—would be labeled as suspect and would almost certainly be blacklisted. Few were willing to allow their careers and futures in the industry to be preventably destroyed, and so virtually all open protest quickly ended.

THE RISE AND FALL OF MCCARTHY

It was at about that time, in the early 1950s, that Senator Joseph McCarthy, a Republican from Wisconsin, came to national attention. He first came into regard in February 1950 with a high-profile charge that the Department of State was infiltrated with Communists. During the next three years he repeatedly accused various high-ranking government officials of subversive activities. Following the 1952 elections, in which the Republicans were elected to the majority party in the Senate, McCarthy became the chairman of the Senate Subcommittee on Investigations, which increased his platform to probe for alleged Communist activities. Then in 1954 he accused the Secretary of the Army, Robert Stevens, and senior U.S. Army officers of concealing foreign espionage activities. That proved to be the beginning of the end of McCarthy's political influence.

McCarthy's army accusations and subsequent hearings aroused the wrath of many military leaders. To discredit McCarthy and the chief counsel of the Senate subcommittee, Roy Cohn, the Army charged that the two of them had sought to obtain special privileges for G. David Schine, a twenty-six-year-old committee aide, prior to and after he was drafted into the Army in November 1953. McCarthy countercharged that these allegations were made in bad faith and were designed to prevent his committee from continuing its probe of Communist subversion in the Army.

These hearings, with their accompanying charges and countercharges, began on April 22, 1954. They were conducted before live TV audiences for thirty-six days and were viewed by an estimated 20 million people. After hearing thirty-two witnesses, a special committee concluded that McCarthy himself had not exercised any improper influence on behalf of David Schine but that Roy Cohn, McCarthy's chief counsel, had engaged in "unduly persistent or aggressive efforts" on behalf of Schine. The committee also concluded that Army secretary Robert Stevens and Army counsel John Adams "made efforts to terminate or influence the investigation and hearings" about the Army subversion.

These hearings, along with McCarthy's increasingly sharp attacks on the Eisenhower administration, eroded support for McCarthy among Republican party leaders and the public at large (even though the 1954 Gallup poll reported that the senator was fourth on its list of most admired men). In June 1954 Senator Ralph Flanders, a Republican from Vermont, introduced a resolution calling for McCarthy's censure; on December 2, following lengthy hearings and debate, the Senate voted sixty-seven to twenty-two to condemn McCarthy for behavior that was "contemptuous, contumacious, and denunciatory" and obstructive of the legislative process. McCarthy remained in the Senate, but he fell into relative political obscurity. He died in office in 1957.

HOLLYWOOD'S RESPONSE

Joseph McCarthy and the HUAC remain highly controversial elements of the 1950s and the early cold war period, but, as can be imagined, there has never been much support for them or their activities in the entertainment industry. It should come as no surprise, then, that many of the Hollywood productions of that time and the years that followed included some sort of direct or symbolic message about those hearings. While many examples of protest pieces can be cited, an obvious example is blacklisted playwright Arthur Miller's play *The Crucible* (1953), which is about the 1692 Salem witch trials but which was intended as an unfavorable reflection of the HUAC and McCarthy hearings.[14]

"Twelve Angry Men" also came to life during this time period. In 1995, Reginald Rose said, "Issues that bother me are issues concerning people who want to impose their beliefs on others. . . . In a way, almost everything I wrote in the fifties was about McCarthy. I was surprised I got away with the stuff I did. Television was so sensitive to criticism, and the criticism almost always came from the right. The network people were really petrified for their jobs. Yet, they were also afraid of being that way, so sometimes things got through."[15]

The McCarthy-Army hearings were televised from April to June 1954. "Twelve Angry Men" was first broadcast on September 20, 1954. In those days scripts were typically produced and aired within one to six months after a playwright submitted his first outline to a network. Clearly, "Twelve Angry Men" was born straight out of the spring 1954 McCarthy hearings. Rose and his audience had had a full diet of those televised hearings. Thus no reader or viewer of "Twelve Angry Men" will properly understand it (or its subsequent film or stage versions) without seeing it in the context of that day's political and cultural events. Juror #8, the liberal-minded hero of "Twelve Angry Men," is the defender of the maligned, misaccused, and downtrodden victim/defendant in the play. The story's white-suited hero (as he is costumed in the 1957 film version) uses calm reason to reveal profound gaps in the charges against the accused. Thus armed, he stands up against the wild-eyed, irrational, and dangerous conservatives on the jury who pursue the powerless victim for their own irresponsible and personal reasons. Juror #8 is not only the defendant's savior, but the savior of democracy. Rose's parallels to the Washington, D.C. hearings are obvious: From his perspective, it was the wild-eyed, irrational, and dangerous conservatives in Congress who pursued the powerless victims in the 1940s and '50s. Sadly, his point goes on, there was no levelheaded, white-clad Juror #8 to stand up for them and protect them from the tyrannical, powerful few within the establishment.

TWELVE ANGRY MEN TODAY

Despite the fact that the HUAC and Joe McCarthy have, for the most part, slipped into being just another chapter in the history books, *Twelve Angry Men* continues to be a respected work of American art. It remains a part of the academic curricula in many secondary schools and universities across the country. Reginald Rose is still sought after for scripts and interviews, being seen as one of the few surviving greats of the Golden Age of Television. And the messages of *Twelve Angry Men* are still considered relevant for today: Fair and impartial juries are important; the rights of the individual need to be respected and defended, regardless of his or her ethnicity or political beliefs; and beware of the dangers of big government and of a powerful few who lose their perspective.

And so out of the 1950s live television dramas—whose time and technology have long gone by—and out of the HUAC and McCarthy hearings—the details of which have faded from memory and can only be retrieved with focused intentionality—*Twelve Angry Men* nonetheless remains. Its script can be—and often is—acquired, read, and performed. Its messages and warnings are still proclaimed, embraced, and hopefully heeded in America's courts and legislative bodies.

NOTES

1. Reginald Rose, *Six Television Plays*. New York: Simon & Schuster, 1956.
2. Quoted in Rex Polier, "Reflections on TV's Golden Age," *Los Angeles Times*, January 1, 1982.
3. "Studio One," *Variety*, September 22, 1954.
4. Rose, *Six Television Plays*.
5. Diane Werts, "Glued to the Tube/Twelve New Angry Men Remake Is a Part of a Return to Provocative Days," *Newsday*, August 12, 1997.
6. Quoted in Polier, "Reflections on TV's Golden Age."
7. Quoted in Tom Stempel, *Storytellers to the Nation: A History of American Television Writing*. New York: Continuum, 1992.

8. Quoted in Stempel, *Storytellers to the Nation.*

9. Quoted in Stempel, *Storytellers to the Nation.*

10. Rose, *Six Television Plays.*

11. Quoted in Robert Strauss, "The Star Never Showed Up . . . and Other Memories of Live TV," *Newsday,* 1997.

12. Quoted in Max Wilk, *The Golden Age of Television.* New York: Delacorte Press, 1976.

13. Quoted in Peter Roffman and Jim Purdy, *The Hollywood Social Problem Film: Madness, Despair, and Politics from the Depression to the Fifties.* Bloomington: Indiana University Press, 1981.

14. It should be noted that there were also many other productions that were intended to "prove Hollywood's loyalty" to Washington, D.C. and the nation. Two examples of those works are *On the Waterfront* (1954), about a once promising boxer (Marlon Brando) who becomes entangled in corrupt union politics and then heroically becomes a police informer, and *The Caine Mutiny* (1954), in which a U.S. Navy ship's executive officer (Van Johnson) bravely but wrongly stands up to his cowardly, incompetent, and paranoid captain (Humphrey Bogart) and saves the ship during a hurricane. The villain in *Caine* is the left wing, intellectual deck officer (Fred MacMurray) who has duped the naïve, liberal executive officer (and his followers) into wrongly rebelling against authority.

15. Quoted in Jeff Kisseloff, *The Box: An Oral History of Television, 1920–1961.* New York: Viking, 1995.

Characters and Plot

Introduction to Characters: One Main Protagonist and Two Main Antagonists

Juror #8: This forty-two-year-old architect is the play's main protagonist. At the opening, he is the lone voice for reason, compassion, and wisdom. The prosecution has apparently presented a heavy-handed, circumstantial case against the frightened and poorly defended nineteen-year-old boy on trial, and of all the jurors, only #8 seriously questions it. He is self-confident (but selfless) and dogged in his convincing of the other jurors, able to stand firm in the face of their often mean-spirited and personal criticism. His liberal-minded compassion makes him clearly more than just the savior of the play's lone disadvantaged defendant. Juror #8 is the defender of the democratic process. Without him—and others like him—the American system of justice could not be trusted to protect the innocent and punish the guilty. He is thoughtful, but he speaks his mind and stands strong for what he believes. Time after time he demonstrates mercy, inclusion, and bridge-building to those who both agree and disagree with him. These are the same qualities that characterize him as the ultimate liberal hero.

Juror #3: In many ways, Juror #3 is just an average working-class citizen. This forty-year-old hard-driving, no-nonsense entrepreneur owns his own messenger service and has enough internal passion not to let anything stand in the way of making his business succeed. Yet those same traits are also probably his greatest weaknesses. As in his business, he is intolerant, difficult, and demanding in the jury room, but in that legal setting those attributes are inappropriate and unsettling. They come out of an angry, self-centered, and prideful core, resulting in overly opinionated, judgmental, critical, and often rude behavior toward others. Not only are those traits out of place in the jury room, but

27

they are out of place in most of his relationships. During the deliberations, he speaks multiple times of his estranged son. He clearly carries hurt and resentment from the decades-old failure of that relationship, but audience members can easily imagine how the son came to be estranged from this unpleasant, even sadistic man. While Juror #3's hurt from his son is no doubt real and valid, it would likely pale if compared with the hurt and anger inflicted by him on to his son. And in establishing his verdict in the jury room, he obviously directs much of his anger for his son against the defendant, a boy whose relationship with his own father is tempestuous.

Juror #4: This antagonist is not exactly a bad man, but he lacks the heart needed to be a good one. A fifty-year-old stockbroker, he certainly seeks the truth in *Twelve Angry Men,* but in a cold unfeeling way. Lacking humanity and compassion in his assessment of the accused, he is quite comfortable with approaching deliberation as an intellectual exercise, not caring that a human life weighs in the balance. Nonetheless, he shares the audience's (and the other jurors') disgust with those jurors who vote for the wrong reasons, regardless of how that vote is cast. It is he who silences Juror #10 in his racist tirade for a guilty verdict. Therefore although he is an antagonist, he is certainly not the enemy.

PLOT SUMMARY

Since *Twelve Angry Men* has been presented in four variants across different media, there is no single version of the play. The best-known version, however, is the 1957 film starring Henry Fonda. The following summary, therefore, reflects that film version.

Twelve Angry Men is the story of a jury deliberating its verdict in the trial of a young, presumably Puerto Rican man (although he is clearly Hispanic, his exact ethnicity is never exactly labeled) who is accused of murdering his father. The story is told in real, contiguous time; there are no time lapses. The ninety-five minutes of action cover that same amount of time in the characters' lives onscreen. Throughout the deliberations, both the jurors and the audience know that if the defendant is found guilty, he will be sentenced to death by the electric chair.

The action is set in New York City during the summer. The

characters deliberate in a stiflingly hot, un-air-conditioned jury room. It has a large rectangular table, twelve wooden chairs that are not especially comfortable, a washroom, and windows along one wall.

The characters dress in everyday business clothes suitable to their stations in life. For example, Jurors #4 (a stockbroker), #8 (an architect), and #12 (an advertising salesman) wear jackets and ties. But Jurors #1 (a high school football coach), #5 (a mechanic), and #6 (a house painter) wear open collars.

After a lengthy and wordless opening in which the audience sees the outside and then the inside of the New York City Court of General Sessions Building, the story begins inside a courtroom with a judge dispassionately charging the jury to deliberate the murder case that it has just heard. As the jurors leave the courtroom, the audience sees the accused, a frightened, non-threatening Hispanic youth, whom the audience later discovers is nineteen years old.

As the jury settles into the jury room, the members make small talk, which reveals early glimpses into their characters. For example, the insecure Juror #2 (a bank clerk) tries to buy friends by offering sticks of gum to the other jurors. The irresponsible Juror #7 (a marmalade salesman) flicks his gum wrapper out the open window and announces his desire to finish quickly because he has baseball tickets to that night's Yankees game. Juror #5, who grew up in the slums, expresses nervous dismay when he discovers the guard locking the jury inside of the jury room. And the insightful Juror #8 thoughtfully looks out the window, presumably already weighing the issues and gravity of the case.

Once settled, the group decides to take a preliminary vote by a show of hands, which dramatically comes out eleven to one in favor of a guilty verdict, with Juror #8 casting the only vote for not guilty. Jurors #3 (head of a messenger service), #7, and #10 (a garage owner) immediately and caustically criticize him, intolerantly demanding why he voted not guilty in light of the perceived convincing evidence for guilty. "Boy-oh-boy," chides Juror #10, "there's always one." Juror #8 responds with mild defensiveness that he's not sure the youth is not guilty but that there is a life at stake and he just wants to talk about it for a bit: "It's not so easy for me to raise my hand and send a boy off to die without talking about it first." Thus begins the lengthy and laborious process of exposing the inner motivations of each juror's vote, and ultimately the changing of those votes.

As discussion begins, Juror #8 reminds the other jurors (and informs the audience) that the accused youth comes from a disadvantaged background, including spending time in an orphanage when his abusive father was in prison. Juror #10 responds incredulously, with underlying racist tones that the defendant's story should not be believed: "You're not going to tell us that we're supposed to believe that kid, knowing what he is. . . . I mean they're born liars."

MAJOR PIECES OF EVIDENCE

The group then agrees to go around the table and present the reasons for their votes. This process reveals that there are three major pieces of evidence against the defendant. First, an old man who lives in the apartment below the victim's apartment had been in bed when he heard impassioned death threats in the apartment above; moments later, he heard a heavy thud of the presumably murdered body falling to the floor. He then claimed to have gotten out of bed and gone to his apartment's front door just in time to have seen the boy run down the stairs and get away. Second, the murder weapon (an unusual switch knife) matches the knife that the storekeeper of a neighborhood "junk shop" testified that he sold to the boy on the night of the murder. The boy agrees that he bought the knife from the storekeeper but says that he lost it through a hole in his trousers pocket before the murder occurred. Third, a woman who lives across the "el" tracks (the elevated train tracks) testified that she witnessed the murder through the windows of a passing train.

In addition, the defendant's alibi is unsupportable. He claimed to have been at the movies at the time of the murder, but he could not remember the movie titles or any of their actors.

Despite the evidence, Juror #8 believes that the case warrants close scrutiny. As the jurors reexamine the evidence, time and time again it is found to be noncredible or inconclusive. The first argument that is challenged is the idea that the defendant had to have committed the murder because on that night he possessed a very unusual knife that exactly matched the murder weapon. Juror #8 produces a knife that matches the murder weapon, dramatically throwing it point-first into the jury room's conference table. He explains that, while out walking a few nights prior, he bought the knife at a pawnshop a few blocks from where the murder occurred, thus effectively discrediting the idea that the boy's knife had to be the murder weapon.

Sensing a small victory, he follows that by offering the other jurors a deal: He proposes a second vote, but this time by secret ballot. If the vote remains eleven to one, he will go along with the majority, and the boy will be found guilty. But if any others vote with him, they will all continue to deliberate. With all in agreement, they vote. The ballot comes in ten votes for guilty, two for not guilty. Angry finger-pointing ensues, but wise old Juror #9 (a retiree) quickly admits to changing his vote, saying of #8, "It's not easy to stand alone against the ridicule of others. So he gambled for support, and I gave it to him. . . . I want to hear more." With one convert, Juror #8 presses forward.

The next major argument considers the testimony of the old man who lived under the scene of the murder. As the discussion develops, Juror #8 points out that the old man could not have heard the murderer's death threats (as he claimed in court) over the noise of the passing "el" train, which the woman who lived across the tracks testified she saw was there as the murder was happening. That is enough to convince Juror #5 to change his vote, followed closely thereafter by Juror #11 (an immigrant watchmaker, assumedly a Holocaust survivor). Then the group reenacts the movement of the old man (who is disabled) getting out of bed and going to the door, where, he testified, he saw the boy run away. Together the jurors conclude that the man could not have gotten to the door in the time he said he did in order to see the murderer get away.

That discussion, with the peripheral arguments and the jury's obvious shift away from a guilty vote, has been getting increasingly bothersome to several of the more entrenched pro-guilty jurors, especially Jurors #3 and #10. At that point, Juror #3 and #8 engage in a heated argument, with Juror #3 exploding in anger and threats when #8 (correctly) calls him a sadist who just wants to see the boy die.

A Tie Vote

Once the group settles down, they agree to another vote by a show of hands. The vote comes in tied six to six, with Jurors #2 and #6 changing their votes. At this point, Juror #10, seeing the "evidence" he put his faith in being countered by other interpretations, bursts forth with exasperation (and irony), "I'm sick and tired of facts. You can twist 'em any way you like. Ya' know what I mean?"

Having successfully cast doubt on one witness's testimony and on the damning nature of a key piece of evidence, Juror #8 raises the question of the defendant's alibi: "An important point for the prosecution was the fact that after the boy claimed he'd been at the movies during the hours the killing took place, couldn't remember the names of the movies or the stars who appeared in them." Juror #4, the coldhearted but truth-seeking intellectual stockbroker, takes up the prosecution's position on this point, and so the dialogue continues between #4 and #8. Juror #8 believes that the stress of having argued bitterly with and been slapped by his father earlier in the evening (which both the defendant and the prosecution had agreed happened) and then having been questioned in his apartment by the police while the body of his dead father was still lying on the floor in the next room would have been enough to make the boy unable to recall relatively minor details such as movie titles and actors' names. Juror #4 is unconvinced: "The boy couldn't remember the names of the movies he saw because he wasn't there that night." Then #8 begins to question #4 as a prosecutor would, asking him about when he went to the movies a few nights prior. While #4 is able to recall some details, he quickly becomes unable to answer questions about titles and actors' names. Reminding Juror #4 (and the audience) that he is under comparatively little stress, Juror #8 makes the point that the boy *could* have been at the movies and forgotten the details as he claimed.

The group's discussion then moves to the topic of the angle of the knife wound. In this suspenseful and richly characterized segment, Juror #3 demonstrates how he would have used the knife had he been the murderer; he would have stabbed overhand and *down* into the victim's chest, which matches what the coroner's report showed actually happened. Yet in pantomiming this to his fellow jurors, he seems to threaten Juror #8 with the knife, and in the process, #3 reveals even further his angry, violence-prone, sadistic inner self. Following that, Juror #5, the young man who grew up in the violent slum (but who has a good heart), shows that an experienced knife fighter like the defendant would have likely used the switch knife to stab under-handed, with the blade pointing *up* into the victim's chest. This further suggests that the man's son may not have been the assailant.

This convincing demonstration by Juror #5 brings up, ar-guably, one of the most pathetic—but magnificently writ-ten—behaviors in play. Juror #7, the crass, sophomoric, ir-responsible, and boastful marmalade salesman, announces, "I don't know about the rest of 'em, but I'm gettin' a little tired of this yakkity-yakkin' back and forth. It's gettin' us nowhere. So I guess *I'll* have to break it up. I change my vote to not guilty." To the disgust of those on both sides of the vote, he cavalierly changes his vote just so the deliberation will end sooner.

A Strong Majority for Not Guilty

Juror #8 follows this by calling for another vote, which the foreman obliges by asking for a show of hands. This time the indecisive foreman and the spineless #12 join with the not guilty voters (even though #12 will have changed his mind three times before finally deciding on not guilty at the play's end). This leaves only the play's three main antagonists voting guilty: Jurors #3, #4, and #10. Juror #10 is furious at the out-come of that vote. He stands and launches into a revolting racist tirade. But as he rants, the other jurors one by one leave the table and stand around the room with their backs to him. Finally he is shunned and alone, as if talking into the wind. Juror #4, whom the audience cannot doubt is ashamed to be voting in agreement with #10, quietly but forcefully confronts him and hisses, "Sit down and don't open your mouth again." Juror #10 is silenced, and the others slowly return to the table.

The ever-inclusive Juror #8 breaks the tension by seeking common ground, as he has throughout the play, and says, "It's always difficult to keep personal prejudice out of a thing like this. Wherever you run into it, prejudice always ob-scures the truth. I don't really know what the truth is. I don't suppose anybody will ever really know." But for the remain-der of the play, Juror #10's physical and emotional en-durance, as well as his influence, is through. He has no more lines, he slinks around in the background, only to nod an approval for a not guilty vote near the end of the film.

With calmer heads back in control, Juror #8 respectfully invites #4 to articulate the remaining guilty voters' reasons for their position. With the intellectualism of a college professor addressing his students, Juror #4 moves the discussion to the testimony of the woman across the "el" tracks who witnessed the murder while she was lying in bed unable to sleep in the heat of the night. Her eyewitness testimony is convincing, even enough for Juror #12 ("bouncin' backwards and forwards like a tennis ball") to temporarily change back to a guilty vote. Yet it is then that the observant Juror #9 remembers that he had seen marks on her nose from wearing eyeglasses (which she did not wear in court). Together (with the exception of Juror #3), the group reasons that (1) she would not have been wearing glasses in bed; (2) according to her own testimony, the length of the murder was not long enough for her to have had time to put on her glasses; and (3) her unaided eyesight is suspect, so they cannot trust that she saw the necessary details clearly enough at a distance of sixty feet. All have now been convinced of a reasonable doubt about the young defendant's guilt, except for Juror #3.

Throughout the play, Juror #3 has made several angry references to his son—"the ungrateful kid!"—and their estranged relationship. Now in the climactic moment of the play, he storms around the room, yelling abuses to and about his fellow jurors ("You lousy bunch of bleeding hearts!"), groping for some way to legitimize his seemingly unsupportable guilty vote. Finally, in rage he pulls his son's photograph which has fallen to the table from his wallet and in fury tears it to pieces. Disabled by his fellow jurors, he is no longer able to hold the young defendant guilty for the hurt he carries from his son. He resignedly crumples to the table, breaks down in tears, and says, "Not guilty."

No more remains to be said or done. After a few respectful moments, the other jurors move quietly toward the door. The foreman knocks, the guard opens the door, and all except #3 and #8 file out. Juror #3 remains seated and broken, and #8 comes to him in silent pastoral compassion. He helps him with his chair, then with his coat, and together they wordlessly leave the jury room.

In the final scene, Jurors #8 and #9—the earliest allies in the jury room—unexpectedly meet on the steps of the courthouse and warmly exchange greetings and names. Yet with no longer anything to say to one another, they part, wishing each other well as they go on about the living of their lives, never to see each other again.

CHAPTER 1

Insights from the Makers of *Twelve Angry Men*

Creating the Original Story

Reginald Rose

In 1956, playwright Reginald Rose published the scripts of six of his television plays, including "Twelve Angry Men," as well as his commentary on each of the plays. In his commentary on "Twelve Angry Men," Rose talks about how he created the script and shares personal reflections on the story.

Twelve Angry Men is certainly [a difficult play] to read. In reading plays, most of which generally are devoid of any descriptive matter whatsoever (outside of brief outlines of the sets), the first task a reader has is that of separating the characters from each other. In most cases, after several pages have been read, the names of the characters in the play have been memorized by the reader, mental images of these characters have been formed, and it is a relatively simple thing to distinguish between the characters and to know, almost automatically, who is speaking each line. In reading *Twelve Angry Men*, however, I realize that it is almost impossible to form immediate and distinct pictures of each of the twelve men, designated as they are only by number. This play was constructed to fall into shape upon being seen, and since I felt that a dozen names would be quite meaningless to a viewing audience (members of a jury rarely address each other by name), I omitted the sometimes annoying chore of selecting names for my characters. . . .

A PLAY RELATED TO PERSONAL EXPERIENCE

Twelve Angry Men is the only play I've written which has any relation at all to actual personal experience. A month or so before I began the play I sat on the jury of a manslaughter case in New York's General Sessions Court. This was my first experience on a jury, and it left quite an impression on

Excerpted from *Six Television Plays*, by Reginald Rose (New York: Simon & Schuster, 1956). Copyright ©1956 by Reginald Rose, renewed 1984. Reprinted by permission of International Creative Management, Inc.

me. The receipt of my jury notice activated many grumblings and mutterings, most of which began with lines like "My God, eight million people in New York and they have to call me!" All the prospective jurors I met in the waiting room the first day I appeared had the same grim, horribly persecuted attitude. But, strangely, the moment I walked into the courtroom to be empaneled and found myself facing a strange man whose fate was suddenly more or less in my hands, my entire attitude changed. I was hugely impressed with the almost frightening stillness of the courtroom, the impassive, masklike face of the judge, the brisk, purposeful scurrying of the various officials in the room, and the absolute finality of the decision I and my fellow jurors would have to make at the end of the trial. I doubt whether I have ever been so impressed in my life with a role I had to play, and I suddenly became so earnest that, in thinking about it later, I probably was unbearable to the eleven other jurors.

It occurred to me during the trial that no one anywhere ever knows what goes on inside a jury room but the jurors, and I thought then that a play taking place entirely within a jury room might be an exciting and possibly moving experience for an audience.

Actually, the outline of *Twelve Angry Men*, which I began shortly after the trial ended, took longer to write than the script itself. The movements in the play were so intricate that I wanted to have them down on paper to the last detail before I began the construction of the dialogue. I worked on the idea and outline for a week and was stunned by the time I was finished to discover that the outline was twenty-seven typewritten pages long. The average outline is perhaps five pages long, and many are as short as one or two pages. This detailed setting down of the moves of the play paid off, however. The script was written in five days and could have been done in four had I not written it approximately fifteen pages too long.

BLENDING FOUR ELEMENTS TOGETHER

In writing *Twelve Angry Men* I attempted to blend four elements which I had seen at work in the jury room during my jury service. These elements are: a) the evidence as remembered and interpreted by each individual juror (the disparities here were incredible); b) the relationship of juror to juror in a life-and-death situation; c) the emotional pattern of each individual juror; and d) physical problems such as the weather, the time, the uncomfortable room, etc. All of these elements are of vital importance in any jury room, and all of them presented excellent dramatic possibilities.

Before I began to plot the play, I felt that the basic problem was going to consist of a constant search for drama and movement in order to prevent a normally static situation from becoming too static. Actually, as it turned out, the writing of *Twelve Angry Men* became a struggle to cram all of the detail, action and character I had devised into the less than fifty minutes of air time available.

Before the play went into rehearsal I had to cut large chunks of dialogue, and, since I was dealing with quite an involved plot, all the cuts were made on passages that had been written to give some depth to the characters. This left the bare frame of the plot and the skeletons of the people. To this day I have not been able to decide whether the cuts made *Twelve Angry Men* more effective or not. The men of the play were easily recognizable as types, but I believe that whatever dimension they had as real people was achieved as much by the excellence of the performance as it was by the personal insights revealed in dialogue. What *Twelve Angry Men* has to say about democracy, justice, social responsibilities and the pressure of the times upon the people who live them has some importance, I believe, and perhaps helps to overshadow the meager development of some of the characters.

As a motion picture, released [in 1957], I think that *Twelve Angry Men* has grown in stature. It is nearly twice as long as the television play, and much of the extra time has been spent in exploring the characters and their motivations for behaving as they do toward the defendant and each other.

The time limitations of television tend to restrict the complete development of a play so that it is necessary to show only brief fragments of people if the plot is fairly involved, or the barest sketch of a plot if the characters are to be fully developed. The only way out of this stifling trap is longer, more expensive shows, of which I, for one, am heartily in favor.

The production problems of *Twelve Angry Men* were, for what seemed like a reasonably simple show, incredibly involved. The set, to be realistic, had to be small and cramped. This, of course, inhibited the movement of cameras and presented director Frank Schaffner with an endless traffic jam which would have had Robert Moses spinning like a ball-bearing top. Somehow, however, Mr. Schaffner managed to capture the speaker of each line on camera at precisely the right moment and composed starkly realistic, tension-filled pictures of the reactions to these lines. This was perhaps the best-directed show I've ever seen on television and Mr. Schaffner won a mantelpieceful of awards for it, including the Christopher Award, the Sylvania Award and the Academy of Television Arts and Sciences Emmy Award.

Twelve Angry Men, incidentally, was the first of my shows to be seen by my two youngsters—Jonathan, then five and a half, and Richard, three. (Since then, two more small twin boys have joined our family!) I hadn't intended to have them see it at all, but one Sunday afternoon they discovered that I had made arrangements to run off a kinescope of the show for some people who had missed it and they begged to be allowed to see it. Never one to resist the accomplished wheedling of small, determined boys, I agreed, provided that they swore up and down to sit like lumps and not utter a sound. They said they would and they kept their word. From time to time I looked at them, two little figures squatting on hassocks, wide-eyed, unmoving, terribly impressed with the entire situation, and I felt, I must admit, a tinge of pride that they were obviously so fascinated with something I had created. At the end of the show, after much small talk, I went over to the hassock where Jonathan still sat, silent and obviously impressed. With what must have been some smugness I asked, "Well, how'd you like it, Jon?"

He looked at me gravely. Then he whispered, "Boy, were they angry!"

He has never mentioned it again, and if he thinks I'm going to ask him. . . .

The Challenges of Screenwriting the 1957 Film Version

Reginald Rose

This article originally appeared in the *New York Times* films section just a few days before the 1957 film version of *Twelve Angry Men* opened. Screenwriter Reginald Rose shares part of the process he went through in creating this story. He writes, "It has without question the most intricate plot of anything I've ever written." And he attributes the success of the plot to the interactions between his carefully constructed characters.

It's true that the screen play is only one of myriad elements that constitute a finished motion picture, but since it happens to be the foundation upon which "12 Angry Men" is built, and since I think the script is something enormously different in the way of motion pictures, it might be interesting to examine the problems inherent in the construction of this particular script.

The film, save for three or four minutes of its running time, takes place entirely in one cramped and stuffy jury room. The action is continuous in time and the twelve jurors are together in this room for about ninety minutes. During this time a very complex story is introduced, developed and resolved by them.

The problem of constructing a script to conform to these given conditions, of making it move and of causing it to produce an emotional as well as intellectual impact became not only an artistic labor, but in part an engineering stunt.

DISSECTING CHARACTERS

First, of course, there had to be twelve characters, so I was faced at the outset with the following relatively simple problems. How old is each of these men, what in general does he look like, and what does he do for a living? Is he married, unmarried, divorced? Is he rich, poor or middle-class? What kind of man is each one of them? What does he think, what does he feel, how does he face life, what are his own personal problems, is he bright, dull, neurotic or well-adjusted, extroverted or withdrawn, mature or infantile? Where was he born? Where does he live? How does he react to any one of a number of given situations?

These questions, and many more, had to be asked and answered before I could sit down to write a word of dialogue. Finally, their attitudes toward the immediate problem they face in the film, the decision they must make that will mean freedom or death to a boy accused of murder, had to be examined and carefully drawn.

Once this had all been accomplished, there was a story, finished but for details, and there were twelve contrasting characters to tell this story. It remained now to fit the people into the story so that each would become a separate instrument for advancing it, yet would do so in terms of his own character.

On the surface I suppose that the juror who comes the closest to what the movies generally consider a hero-type is juror No. 8, the part played by Henry Fonda. Yet even this man, in his relentless quest for what he considers to be justice, displays certain qualities that remove him, I trust, from the confines of the cliché hero.

Although "12 Angry Men" takes place in one room, it has without question the most intricate plot of anything I've ever written. From the moment I set down the first word of the screen play the job became one of pitting character against character in such a way that their natural reaction to conflict brings out the proper elements of the plot in proper order. When the first real antagonism appears between two jurors, it is between juror No. 10 (Ed Begley), a garage owner, who feeds his starved ego on his hatred of minorities, and Fonda.

ALL TOP ROLES

Each of the twelve men is used importantly in this film, whether he is characterized as a leader or a follower, a creator of ideas or a listener. Two of the jurors, for instance, the foreman (Martin Balsam) and juror No. 10 (Ed Begley), are deeply involved in the interchange of ideas that formulates

SCREENPLAY FOR *TWELVE ANGRY MEN* DISCOURAGES CRITICISM

François Truffaut (1932–1984), French motion-picture director and critic, writes that Twelve Angry Men *is a film that makes itself more difficult to turn away from as the story unfolds.*

There's the screenplay. Let's talk about it. It's clever, in the best sense of the word, and we at the *Cahiers* don't have much use for movies constructed on good ideas, on astuteness, ingenuity. Still, the script of *Twelve Angry Men* discourages criticism: 1) we are present at a deliberation with a strict continuity of time, place, and action, and experience intensely the feeling, not of something done, but of something being done. It's a triumph of the television style; 2) the stereotyping of the jurors is so nuanced that instead of twelve "specimens," we have only six, each represented twice: two intellectuals, two laborers, two bigots, two smokers, two scrupulous types, two who are absolutely "proper." Each character trades details with an almost identical counterpart, rather than displaying the broad and somewhat strained strokes that are usual in this sort of "conflict cinema."

Many films (some of the best) are boring and make you feel as if you might want to leave to get a drink or look for an available woman. This movie makes it increasingly more difficult to leave as the story unfolds; a man's life is at stake, and only a unanimous verdict can save him from death. One by one the jurors relent under the urgent pleading of Henry Fonda, until only the most obdurate remains unmoved. You're surprised to find yourself rooting for him in the darkness. The last three jurors give in together. What a fantastic idea it was—the most hesitant one changes his mind, becoming a lever on the other two, thus making a verdict of "not guilty" possible.

François Truffaut, *The Films in My Life*, 1978.

the plot of this film, yet their behavior has a subtle influence on the behavior of the other ten men and on the constantly changing pattern of the voting. Much of the intricate business of living is singled out and held up for scrutiny in this jury room, I feel. For instance, the alliances formed for purely intellectual reasons and those formed for emotional reasons alone remind us of larger and more important alliances that we can see at every turn in our newspapers, locally, nationally, internationally.

What finally came out of this very involved creative process are two elements: one, an interesting group of characters; and two, a suspenseful story. Both of these play against each other to create element number three, a screen play that has been made, I believe, into a very provocative motion picture. Final judgment on it must, of course, be left to those who step up to the box office and buy their tickets. But I must say that four small boys who live in our house in a welter of cracker crumbs, marbles and band-aids have told me it is great. They haven't seen it yet, but I'm with them.

The Challenges of Directing the 1957 Film Version

Sidney Lumet, interviewed by *Life*

Sidney Lumet is a well-respected director capable of effectively and seamlessly pulling various elements together in a film. In a 1957 *Life* magazine interview, he speaks of the difficulties of shooting sequences and establishing camera angles in the claustrophobic setting of a jury room for the 1957 film version of *Twelve Angry Men*. Lumet worked extensively in television in the 1950s and directed many of Reginald Rose's teleplays (though he did not direct the 1954 broadcast of "Twelve Angry Men," which was directed by Franklin Schaffner). *Twelve Angry Men* was his first full-length film, and it earned him an Academy Award nomination for best director; it also established him as a director skilled at adapting theatrical works to film. Since then his films have received more than fifty Academy Award nominations. Over his career, he has directed nearly fifty films and produced, written, or acted in more than a dozen others.

Keeping his camera focused on these wrathy faces, a young director, [then] 32-year-old Sidney Lumet, has invaded movies from television and smashed the rules. With Henry Fonda as producer and star, he has made a movie, *Twelve Angry Men*, that hardly moves. It centers in one room and stays at one table. Shortly after the start he gives the ending away. In fact Lumet has done everything usually wrong— and come up with a movie being released by United Artists that is wonderfully right. Building suspense through conflicts and tensions in his 12, he tells an exciting story of a jury battling to a verdict in a murder case. The telling of it nearly drove Lumet out of his mind.

Excerpted from "Good Men and True and All Angry," by Sidney Lumet, *Life*, April 22, 1957. Reprinted by permission of Sidney Lumet.

44

DIFFICULTIES OF DIRECTING

"When you shoot a movie that is nothing but 12 men's faces as they talk angrily to one another and you shoot it out of sequence and the camera is being moved from one angle to another around a room, then," says Sidney Lumet, director of *Twelve Angry Men*, "you go elaborately nuts trying to be consistent about who is looking where and at whom.

"In making *Angry Men* the camera went around the table, shooting chair by chair. Once lights and camera were pointed at a chair, then every speech, no matter its order in the movie, was shot. That meant that often you had only two or three actors in or near chairs, talking and arguing across the table with actors who were not there. You had to figure out where the nonexistent actor's eyes would be, so that the existent actor could stare him down.

"I spent nights puzzling the problem and my script became a maze of diagrams. We had arguments on the set as people tried to explain to me that I was crazy. But the diagrams came out right 396 times in 397 scenes. One we had to reshoot because I had the stockbroker looking the wrong way as he spoke to another actor.

"Then there was the sweat. The movie starts on a hot, humid day and the actors sweat but not equally. The little bank clerk sweats very little. That is in character. The broker, as the wealthy, superior sort of juror, sweats not at all. Then a storm comes up, the weather cools and they all dry off except the messenger service chief. So with every scene we stood before the actor with an atomizer trying to figure out whether or not to squirt on sweat and, if so, just how much to squirt.

"We did all we could honestly do on a one-set movie to heighten the drama. We created a claustrophobic tension by gradually changing camera lenses to narrow the room and crowd up the table. Little by little we lowered the camera level to shoot up at the furious jurymen. And the rate of changes in camera angles is stepped up as the talk grows louder and fiercer."

All of these procedures add greatly to *Twelve Angry Men*, but the film's basic strength lies in a first-rate story by Reginald Rose and fine performances by the actors—E.G. Marshall's frozen-faced stockbroker, Ed Begley's angry, bigoted garage owner, Jack Warden's impatient salesman, Lee J. Cobb's hate-filled messenger service chief, and Henry Fonda's gentle architect who leads the 12 to a just verdict.

Filming *Twelve Angry Men* on a Single Set

Boris Kaufman

Boris Kaufman, A.S.C. (1906–1980), was an experienced cinematographer by the time he worked on
Twelve Angry Men. Polish-born and the brother of
two Soviet film directors, he was the director of photography on twenty-four films spanning four decades
(1930–1970). In this 1956 article, he writes about the
two major and unique difficulties of filming this
movie. The first problem was how to keep the photography from becoming static in this basically one-
set picture. The second was how to present cinematographically the psychological study of twelve men
whose only common denominator was that each was
a juror deciding the life or death of another man.

The ever-present challenge for the director of photography is
how to give each new picture a new and different camera
treatment—a fresh viewpoint, camera-wise. Lest he repeat
himself and fall back on old techniques, the cinematographer
is continually challenged to dig deep into his bag of tricks so
that his photographic technique does not become stagnant.

Sometimes an assignment is filled with more problems
and difficulties than others, as in the case of "12 Angry
Men," which I photographed in 1956 for Orion-Nova Productions in New York. Just one look at the script convinced
me that here was truly a challenging assignment—pho-
tographing a dramatic story within the confines of a single,
one-room set.

The story concerned twelve men who, as jurors, find
themselves locked inside a jury room where they must decide whether a young boy, on trial for his life, is to live or die.
Considering the one-set limitations, the first and most important problem was how to keep the photography of this

picture from becoming static; the entire story was to be staged and photographed in a room no larger than an average hotel room.

The second problem was how to present cinematographically the psychological study of twelve men, each from a different social strata of a big city and whose only common denominator was that he had suddenly found himself in a jury room, and was being asked to pass judgment on the guilt of another human being.

THE ONE-SET LIMITATIONS

The first problem presented the biggest challenge. I had experienced this type of a problem before in one or two pictures, but in a much more fleeting way—for perhaps a sequence or two. But here the entire story was straightjacketed inside a one-room set. Inside a jury room, in which sat twelve men, whose backgrounds, attitudes, problems, and reasons behind their decisions had to be shown photographically as well as in the dialogue.

After much thought and discussion, we decided there was only one way to overcome the possibility of static cinematography. That was to turn the disadvantage of the single set into a pictorial advantage. We decided to use the camera to play up the feeling of confinement and thus contribute dramatically to the total expression of the story, making the confinement an integral pictorial part of the mood.

In good cinematography the camera should never distract the audience from the basic theme and never move without justification. And yet the static condition inherent in the one-set limitations of this story had to be overcome.

The camera had to reveal at the outset the basic character of each man, and his personality traits had to be elaborated upon later in the film to reveal the inner psychological reasons for his behavior.

Because of this the opening scene was the longest, single continuous take I have ever done in all my years as a cinematographer. It ran for seven consecutive minutes. It was made up of 18 separate camera movements which actually showed 18 basic fact situations. It also established the basic style and mood of the picture.

During this seven-minute take the camera introduces the twelve men in a very casual way as they bump into each other and exchange casual remarks which are not at all related to the case on trial. Yet in this way each character immediately begins to relate to every other man in the room and to the story.

ONE DIRECT CONTINUING STORY

From the moment the foreman calls for the first vote we are caught up in a tight, tense drama which never breaks until the end of the film. The screening time is exactly equal to the actual time depicted in the story. Thus, in the hour and one-half the jury spends in the jury room it was impossible to break away from the continuity of the story, to flash back, or attempt a time-lapse. There was nothing for the camera to do except to show one direct continuing story carried further and further along inside the small, hot, locked room.

This picture was shot only one way, to be edited only one way. We didn't "protect" ourselves in the usual way, but decided on the spot how the sequence was to be shot.

Therefore, each angle was checked to determine the best composition with respect to the visual impression we were seeking, and to the action involved. So that when it came time to roll the camera, everybody concerned knew exactly what they were going to do.

The directing technique employed stemmed to a great degree from Sidney Lumet's television background—where, because you are only allowed one take during the actual show, everything is ironed out during rehearsal. Which, when you have as fine and sensitive a feel for camera-work as Lumet, plus his talent and memory for details, combined with a tight script by Reginald Rose, and sensitive performers like Henry Fonda, Lee J. Cobb, Jack Warden, and others in the cast, can prove to be a very successful method of filming a motion picture.

MOOD LIGHTING

There was another pictorial technique we used to emphasize changes in the mood of the story and in the interlocking themes of the plot. This was in the basic lighting patterns, three in all.

First, the lighting suggests bright daylight as the hot afternoon sun shines through the windows as the jury files into the room.

The second stage is reached when the action in the room becomes tight and charged with the oppressive heat of the summer day; the camera moves in again and again to show the tense, electric undercurrents related to the drama going on between the men of the jury. This effect is then heightened by darkening skies in the background, a sudden darkness in the room, and the sound of thunder off in the distance.

FILMING IN JUST ONE ROOM COULD BE AN ADVANTAGE

Director Sidney Lumet discusses how he used multiple lenses and angles to create the illusion that the jury room seemed to get smaller and smaller.

It never occurred to me that shooting an entire picture in one room was a problem. In fact, I felt I could turn it into an advantage. One of the most important dramatic elements for me was the sense of entrapment those men must have felt in that room. Immediately, a "lens plot" occurred to me. As the picture unfolded, I wanted the room to seem smaller and smaller. That meant that I would slowly shift to longer lenses as the picture continued. Starting with the normal range (28 mm to 40 mm), we progressed to 50 mm, 75 mm, and 100 mm lenses. In addition, I shot the first third of the movie above eye level, and then, by lowering the camera, shot the second third at eye level, and the last third from below eye level. In that way, toward the end, the ceiling began to appear. Not only were the walls closing in, the ceiling was as well. The sense of increasing claustrophobia did a lot to raise the tension of the last part of the movie. On the final shot, an exterior that showed the jurors leaving the courtroom, I used a wide-angle lens, wider than any lens that had been used in the entire picture. I also raised the camera to the highest above-eye-level position. The intention was to literally give us all air, to let us finally breathe, after two increasingly confined hours.

Sidney Lumet, *Making Movies*, 1995.

And finally, the pictorial effect of a rainstorm which pours down on the city, and breaks the tension within the room at the height of the emotional battle that has been going on for over an hour and a half. The camera makes the most of the effect of the sight and sound of rain beating against windowpanes, raising the tension of the jurors to the highest point as the last of them finally admits there is room for doubt. The storm breaks only after the jurors' fateful decision has been made.

As we cut to the exterior of the courthouse, with a wet column heavy in the foreground, the men of the jury disperse into the city and the anonymity of the crowd with nothing more to remind us of the drama that took place behind the closed doors of the jury room. Except the coming of night and the wet pavement as the "12 Angry Men" fade into darkness.

Producing and Releasing the 1957 Film

Henry Fonda, as told to Howard Teichmann

Henry Fonda both starred in and coproduced (with screenwriter Reginald Rose) *Twelve Angry Men* (1957). He chose to do this film because he believed it was a film of substance. Yet he came to despise the producer's role on many counts, as described in this excerpt from his autobiography, as told to Howard Teichmann.

12 Angry Men had been a television program written by Reginald Rose. Fonda saw it in a Hollywood projection room, and when United Artists urged him to make the TV show into a movie, he went them one step better and agreed to produce it.

In an art form called theater, in an industry named movies, in a world which for a lengthy time thrived on fads and style, Fonda always looked for substance. He found it in *The Grapes of Wrath*, *The Ox-Bow Incident*, *Mister Roberts*, *The Caine Mutiny Court-Martial*. Now he believed he could reach it again with *12 Angry Men*.

Returning to New York, he contacted the author and learned that Reginald Rose had cut twenty minutes from his original teleplay. No need existed to pad the screenplay. Next, Fonda engaged a young director, Sidney Lumet, and together they interviewed actors. In addition to Fonda the remaining eleven included Lee J. Cobb, Ed Begley, E.G. Marshall, Jack Warden, Martin Balsam, Jack Klugman, and Robert Webber.

The entire action of the film took place in a jury room. Fonda, accustomed to theater work, had the cast rehearse just as it would for a Broadway play. During the two weeks the actors worked on their parts, Lumet, eager to make good on his first film, and his Academy Award–winning cameraman Boris Kaufman moved constantly through the room setting up shots.

INITIAL DISSATISFACTION

"Fonda came into the project a little uptight," Lumet said. "He had to deal with problems he didn't want to deal with. I knew rehearsals were going very well, but two or three days before shooting, I could feel his tension building. One afternoon we stood at the elevator. He turned to me abruptly and with marked irritation said he was dissatisfied with everything. My heart leaped. The star, the producer was unhappy.

"We walked into the studio. Only worklights were on. Hank went pale. The exterior was a shot of the other buildings outside the courthouse in Foley Square. Now, we could have had a huge photo blowup made, but this was a low-budget picture, so we opted for a compromise, a painted backdrop from a photograph. It didn't look great hanging there. You could see all the paint marks."

"Christ!" Fonda exploded before the director. "When I worked with [Alfred] Hitchcock the backings were so real you'd walk into them because you thought they were three dimensional."

"My heart sank," Lumet continued. "I've been told it'll work, Hank."

"You've been told. I tell you it looks terrible! Christ, I don't want to be a fucking producer."

After Fonda left the cameraman assured Lumet that with the proper lighting the drop would look genuine.

"We started shooting the following morning in Manhattan," Lumet said. "The first shot was a very complicated one, over the blades of the fan from a crane. The lighting turned out to be a phenomenal problem. We waited from eight-thirty to four in the afternoon. Hank doesn't sweat, but that was about as close as he's ever come."

INTO THE RUSHES

"We went to the rushes [the preliminary viewing of the film's scenes] the next noon, and he said, 'Sidney, what am I going to do? I can't stand seeing myself on the screen. I never go to rushes, and sometimes I wait two years to see a finished film I've made. Sometimes I never see them.'

"Hank steeled himself, walked into the projection room and sat down behind me. He watched for a while, and then he put his hand on the back of my neck and squeezed so hard I thought my eyes would pop out. He leaned forward and said quietly, 'Sidney, it's magnificent.' Then he dashed out and never came to the rushes again.

"What is so fascinating to me about Fonda as a talent is I don't think if you took a stick and beat him he could do anything false, he's incapable. As a performer, as a man, he's pure. He's like a barometer of truth on the set. Fonda has the inner resource to make the lines deeply true. Great actor. I don't use that term often."

ELEANOR ROOSEVELT COMMENTS ON *TWELVE ANGRY MEN*

In her widely circulated newspaper column My Day, *Eleanor Roosevelt wrote her reaction to the 1957 film* Twelve Angry Men. *Her opposition to the death penalty was well known; she believed that in most cases it was nearly impossible for a jury to be absolutely sure of a suspect's guilt. The following column excerpt appeared on April 20, 1957.*

The other night I saw a private showing of Henry Fonda in "Twelve Angry Men." He is magnificent, but the whole cast is made up of excellent actors.

As a character study, this is a fascinating movie, but more than that, it points up the fact, which too many of us have not taken seriously, of what it means to serve on a jury when a man's life is at stake. In addition, it makes vivid what "reasonable doubt" means when a murder trial jury makes up its mind on circumstantial evidence.

Eleanor Roosevelt, *My Day. Vol. 3, First Lady of the World*, David Elmblidge, ed., 1991.

"I hired Sidney," Fonda says, "because he had the reputation of being wonderful with actors. We got a bonus that nobody counted on. He also had incredible organization and awareness of the problem of shooting and not wasting time."

It required seventeen days to get the action of *12 Angry Men* onto the celluloid. The film Fonda produced came in at a ridiculously low three hundred and forty thousand dollars, a thousand dollars under budget.

"Rose, Lumet, and I realized we had something special when we saw the first rough cut," Fonda says. "We dreamed of putting it into a small East Side movie house, the kind that held a few hundred people at the most, and we hoped that word of mouth would spread just as it had built with Paddy Chayefsky's *Marty*."

FIRST PUBLIC SHOWING

"Well, that never happened. I got a phone call from the head of United Artists, Arthur Krim. 'What're you doing? We want you. Get down here just as fast as you can.'

"When I got down to Krim's office," Fonda continues, "there sat Bob Benjamin and the other heads of the Loew's Circuit. They'd seen our picture and they'd flipped out. They wanted it for Easter Week for all of their flagship theaters across the country. I told 'em I'd like to think on it a while."

"Are you out of your ever-loving mind?" Krim thundered. "All you'll have to do is sit back and hire people to take the wheelbarrows of money to the bank."

As United Artists had put up the financing for the film, Fonda felt he had no alternative.

"The Capitol Theater was Loew's flagship in New York," Fonda says. "It's been gone for some time now, but in case anyone's forgotten, it had over forty-six hundred seats. The opening day *12 Angry Men* barely filled the first four or five rows. They pulled it after a week."

Henry Fonda decided never to produce a picture again. He thought the failure would be a reflection on him at the box office. There was no second release for his film. No third release either. Could it be that he, too, might suffer irreparable harm?

And then *12 Angry Men* was shown at the Berlin Film Festival. It won first prize. It won prizes in Japan, Australia, Italy, Scandinavia. Krim and Benjamin had been wrong. Fonda, Rose, Lumet, the movie critics, and the public had been right. Fonda breathed with relief.

CHAPTER 2

Scholarly Analysis of *Twelve Angry Men*

READINGS ON
TWELVE ANGRY MEN

Twelve Angry Men Endorses Pluralism and Consensus

Peter Biskind

The jurors in *Twelve Angry Men* represent a spectrum of liberal and conservative views held by Americans in the 1950s. According to Peter Biskind, an alliance between liberals and conservatives would have been inconceivable in the politically and economically unstable 1930s. But in the prosperous 1950s, American centrists (seen in Jurors #8 and #4) formed bands in the name of pluralism, overcoming political extremists (Jurors #3 and #10) and ultimately controlling the political landscape through consensus-building. Biskind is the former executive editor of *Premiere* and former editor-in-chief of *American Film.* He is the author of three books, one of which is the source of this essay.

We are presented with a shot of the massive façade of the Supreme Court Building in New York's Foley Square. The camera slowly crawls up the stone columns to the pediment above. Carved across it in bold letters are the words: "The administration of justice is the firmest pillar of good government." Ninety minutes later we will have seen justice served, and know that in the United States, government is indeed good. The Supreme Court Building is a monument, like the Lincoln and Jefferson memorials that are "quoted" in so many films, and as we look up with the camera at the majestic inscription over our heads, we realize that this will be a film that legitimates an American institution: the criminal justice system.

When the camera takes us inside a small, dingy room, we see a man staring moodily out the window at the steep sides of the skyscrapers beyond. The man is Henry Fonda, the film is Sidney Lumet's *12 Angry Men* (1957), and we are about to sit in on the deliberations of a jury. As the film unreels, we notice that the characters don't have names. And when one wryly says to another, after a particularly acrimonious exchange, "Nice bunch'a guys," and the latter replies, "I guess they're the same as any," we realize that these figures are symbols, standing for everyone, and that the film, more than legitimating this or that institution, is after bigger game. It will legitimate a process. For society to work, it was not only necessary that Americans hold certain beliefs in common, but that they agree on the mechanics of reaching agreement. The jury, with its frequent straw votes, its tug-of-war between opposing perspectives, its give-and-take, its stress on conciliation, on integrating clashing points of view, and its imperative of unanimity, was particularly well suited to dramatizing this process.

The defendant in *12 Angry Men* is an eighteen-year-old, apparently Hispanic youth who is charged with stabbing his father to death. (I say "apparently," because although the film suggests that the defendant is a member of a minority group, it is a bit coy about saying just which one. Like the jurors, he is a "symbol"; he stands for all of them.) There is strong circumstantial evidence against him. The downstairs neighbor heard him threatening his father, heard the thud of the body against the floor, and saw the boy run downstairs immediately after the murder. The son admitted to owning a knife identical to the murder weapon, a switchblade with an unusual, intricately carved handle found sticking out of his father's chest. He implausibly claimed he had lost the knife before the murder, and further told police he was at the movies at the time of the killing, but when pressed by the prosecution, he couldn't remember the names of the movies or anything about them. The circumstantial case is apparently clinched by an eyewitness: a woman living directly across from the apartment of the murdered man on the other side of the elevated subway tracks. She claims she saw the boy kill his father through the window. Finally, to add insult to injury, the defendant has a long record of muggings, car thefts, and so on. But we know there must be something wrong, because in one extended close-up of the boy in the courtroom, before the jury retires, we see that he doesn't look like a murderer; on the contrary, he looks sensitive, soulful, and unhappy.

In view of the strong case against the defendant, it is not too surprising that the jury's first straw vote comes out 11 to 1 for conviction. The sole dissenting vote is cast by the hero, Henry Fonda. It's not that he's certain the boy is innocent; he's just not certain he's guilty. "It's not so easy to raise my hand and send a boy off to die without talking about it first," he says.

HARD-LINERS AGAINST THE ACCUSED

Fonda's dissent doesn't sit so well with the other jurors, for whom it's an open-and-shut case. Three of them take a hard line against the accused. We know they're bad guys even before they open their mouths. One, a salesman (Jack Warden), noisily chews gum, flicks the wrapper out the window, and sits on, not at, the conference table. He has tickets to the ball game that night and is anxious to have the deliberations over and done with so that he can get there in time for the first pitch. "The kid's dangerous; you could see it," he says. Another, a self-made businessman, Ed Begley, has a bad cold and keeps blowing his nose with a flourish of soiled handkerchief. "Human life doesn't mean as much to them as it does to us," he says between snuffles. We know yet another self-made businessman is bad news, because he's played by Lee J. Cobb, who always is, and because he too sits on the table, talks too loud, and is among the first to take off his coat in the sweltering heat. Cobb doesn't even think the boy should have been given a trial. "That's the system," he snarls, in his gravelly voice, "but I'm telling you, sometimes I think we'd be better off if we took these tough kids and slapped 'em down hard *before* they make trouble." All three have already made up their minds, and they have nothing but contempt for the jury process. A fourth juror, E.G. Marshall, is a neatly dressed stockbroker who wears the kind of wire-rimmed granny glasses later made fashionable by Robert McNamara. We know he's a cut above the others because he doesn't sit on the table, but primly in his seat, and despite the heat, he keeps his jacket on. Nevertheless, he shares their dim view of the defendant. "Children from slum backgrounds are potential menaces to society," he says. The remaining seven jurors are fence-sitters, leaning first one way and then the other.

PUZZLING INCONSISTENCIES

Despite the apparent strength of the evidence, there are some puzzling inconsistencies. Why did the boy return to the scene of the crime later that night if he indeed murdered his father? Could the woman across the way really have seen what she said she saw, when there was a train passing between the victim's apartment and her own exactly at the moment of the murder? As Fonda tugs at the loose ends, the prosecution's case begins to unravel, and it becomes obvious that the jurors will not be able to reach a quick decision. Under the press of the summer heat, tempers flare and the debate turns rancorous. The purpose of the deliberations, which is a straightforward, purely practical one—the determination of the guilt or innocence of the defendant—is forgotten, and the differences between Fonda and the others escalate into a battle to the death between irreconcilable principles, making it much more difficult to reach an agreement. In other words, the question at issue is obscured by a cloud of ideology; it has become politicized. "What is it, Love Your Underprivileged Brother Week, or something?" Cobb bellows at Fonda, smacking his lips like a beached flounder. "You come in here with your heart bleeding all over the floor about slum kids and injustice. Everyone knows the kid is guilty. He's got to burn." As Cobb, Begley, and Warden shout and carry on, they sweat like pigs, and even as we watch, dark, ugly rings appear under their armpits. They are erratic, excitable, and irrational, leaping about, frantic with anger, always on the verge of losing control. "I'll kill you, I'll kill you!" thunders Cobb, threatening Fonda with a knife. He has no desire to debate or compromise with those who disagree with him. He just wants to destroy them.

As Fonda and Cobb go at it, the dialogue, plot, physical presentation of characters, and placement of the camera all make us sympathize with Fonda, make us see the issues his way, through his eyes. In contrast to Cobb et al., Fonda is cool as a cucumber; throughout Cobb's tirades, he sits calm and collected in his pale cord suit, like Marshall, declining to remove his jacket until well into the last reel. Moreover, he is mild and reasonable. Despite the fact that he initially defies the others, he is not out to polarize the group; rather, he tries to bring them together, convince them he's right. He is not content to splinter the original, false majority against him; he wants to fashion a new, true majority. Luckily, he has the "facts" on his side. As he analyzes the prosecutor's case, it turns out that both witnesses, the downstairs neighbor and the woman across the way, lied on the stand. Then he demonstrates that the boy's alibi is not so implausible as it sounded at first blush. These facts are enough to convert those who are poorer, weaker, and possibly to the left of himself: a refugee, presumably Jewish, from the Holocaust; a garage mechanic, presumably working-class; and a house painter. With these jurors in tow, Fonda proceeds to forge an alliance with the Wall Street stockbroker, E.G. Marshall. Marshall has been embarrassed by the antics of Cobb and his friends, but since he in essence agrees with their point of view, he has not been able to disavow them. According to Reginald Rose's script, however, "The stockbroker is a man of logic, a man without emotional attachment to the case," and therefore Fonda is able to convince him that the defendant is innocent.

LIBERALS AND CONSERVATIVES MADE COMMON CAUSE

The relative ease with which Fonda brings Marshall over to his point of view indicates that the two men play by the same rules, speak the same language. But this in itself is somewhat of a surprise. Why should they, in fact, share the same assumptions? After all, Fonda, the "bleeding heart," is a liberal, afflicted by the liberal's characteristic compassion for the victim, while Marshall, with his decidedly illiberal attitudes toward the defendant, is considerably to the right of him. In the thirties, during the New Deal, when an alliance of leftists and liberals, Communists and Democrats, faced an alliance of rightists and conservatives, reactionaries and Republicans, across the abyss of the Depression, Fonda and Marshall would have been enemies. But times had changed. This was the fifties, the decade in which it seemed that the United States had solved most of the basic problems of modern industrial society. The miracle of the economy, the seemingly endless flow of consumer goods, the constant technological innovation, ironically promised to realize Marx's dream of a harmonious, classless society, not in the Soviet Union, but right in the heart of capitalist America. The thirties, in other words, were obsolete, and the political alignments that characterized them had shifted dramatically. Liberals and conservatives made common cause against leftists and rightists; the center turned on the extremes. As David Riesman and Nathan Glazer put it, "What happened is that the old issues died, and on the new issues former friends or allies have become enemies, and former enemies have become friends. Thus: liberal intellectuals have had to switch their attitudes towards Wall Street—symbolizing both the great financiers and the giant corporations they organize—and towards 'small business.'" "Liberal intellectuals" and "Wall Street" had become "natural allies."[1]

For its part, Wall Street was quick to respond to love calls from the left with cooing noises of its own. It realized that the New Deal reforms of "that man" (FDR) had saved capitalism, not buried it, that unions were here to stay, and that labor, with an assist from the witch-hunt, had traded in its vision of a socialist future for a car, a television, and a house in Levittown. In other words, if labor accepted the capitalist framework, capital reciprocated by agreeing to play by the rules of the game that had been laid down by the New Deal. Thus, when Eisenhower took over from Truman in 1953, far from rolling back New Deal reforms like social security and unemployment insurance, as some conservatives and most reactionaries had hoped, his administration accepted and consolidated them, gave them the imprimatur of the business community.

The components of this new alliance were the moderate wing of the Democratic Party, the so-called "cold-war liberals"—an assortment of disillusioned ex-Communists, old New Dealers, and social democrats who wholeheartedly embraced the cold war—bankers and lawyers like Averell Harriman and Dean Acheson, along with intellectuals like Daniel Bell, Arthur Schlesinger, Jr., Sidney Hook, and David Riesman. Their counterparts to the right were the "corporate capitalists," the left wing of the Republican Party, made up of the liberal business and financial leaders of the big East Coast, northern, and midwestern-based banks and corporations. The Truman (and later Stevenson) Democrats and Eisenhower Republicans played at the game of electoral politics, but it was this "corporate-liberal" alliance of the center, this "bipartisan" coalition of moderates from both parties, who made up the rules of the game.

12 Angry Men follows this script quite closely. It is, in some sense, a film written by ideology. Although its nameless cast of characters are meant to be just plain folks, fifties Everymen, they actually correspond to clearly defined political types. Fonda, an architect by profession, constructs the alliance of moderates. We know he is a liberal, but we can be much more precise than that. We don't find out anything about his views on Communism or the witch-hunt, but we can also determine that he is a "cold-war liberal" precisely because he is engaged in building a bridge to those to the right of himself and bringing those to the left along with him. Stockbroker Marshall is, of course, the enlightened corporate capitalist, the symbol of Riesman and Glazer's "Wall Street." The understanding between Fonda and Marshall forms the backbone of the corporate-liberal alliance of the center.

THE COMMON LANGUAGE OF PLURALISM

The common language Fonda and Marshall speak was called pluralism. Pluralists believed that America was composed of a diversity of interest groups which competed on a more or less equal basis for a piece of the pie. Like the various blocs of jurors in *12 Angry Men,* they could adjust their differences by reasoning together, if they would only avoid ideologizing their conflicts. With the example of Nazi Germany and Communist Russia fresh in their minds, fifties corporate liberals blamed ideology for polarizing societies, pitting one class or ethnic group against another, thereby rendering democracy unworkable. It was the glory of America that in the fifties, ideology was dead. As Schlesinger summed it up: "The thrust of the democratic faith is away from fanaticism; it is towards compromise, persuasion, and consent in politics, towards tolerance and diversity in society."[2] But the corporate liberals' obituary for ideology was premature. It was alive and well, dwelling where we had looked for it least, in the end-of-ideology ideology of the corporate liberals. It was pluralism itself.

Unlike Marshall, Cobb and his friends are old-fashioned ideologues. They don't care about the language of fact. Or, to put it another way, as Fonda continues to argue with them, we gradually see the ground shift from a dispute over the facts of the case to a dispute over the importance of facts per se. At the beginning of the film, as we have seen, Cobb et al. claim the facts for themselves. "I just want to talk about the facts," says Cobb. "You can't refute the facts." At this point, the facts seem to indict the defendant. Two witnesses, a motive, an alibi like Swiss cheese, apparent possession of the murder weapon, and a long criminal record, all say he's guilty. The facts seem to speak for themselves. "What's there to talk about? Nobody had to think twice except you," Warden complains to Fonda. Cobb derisively calls Fonda "preacher" and berates him for pandering to the passions of the jurors with emotional appeals. By the end of the film, the facts are on the other foot. The bleeding hearts have the facts on their side. "I don't think the kind of boy he is has anything to do with it," says one juror. "The facts are supposed to determine the case." In contrast, Cobb et al. are convicted of emotionalism. When Cobb assures the other jurors, "I have no personal feelings about this," it's just not true. His passionate outbursts, and his refusal to throw in his lot with the developing majority, are signs of psychological imbalance. His problem is his relationship with his son. In the final scene, this emerges as the true reason for his hatred of the defendant, and Cobb nearly has a nervous breakdown. And by this time, Fonda has succeeded in persuading his opponents to accept this framework. They dismiss the facts, ceding them to Fonda and friends. "I'm sick of the facts," admits Begley. "You can twist 'em any way you like." Bereft of facts, Cobb et al. are content to fall back on intuition, on feeling, on subjectivity. They just *know* the boy is guilty.

In the same way that Fonda seizes the ground of fact from Cobb, so pluralists fought to secure the rights to reality from their enemies. In the forties, Lionel Trilling wrote that the future historian of the fifties, undertaking to describe the assumptions of his culture, "will surely discover that the word *reality* is of central importance in his understanding of us." Trilling knew what he was talking about, because he and others like him played a key role in prescribing just what could legitimately be considered "real" in the fifties. Pluralists were quite clear about what reality was not, but they were rather vague about what it was. They would say no more than that reality was complex, ambiguous, and mysterious. Trilling, for example, praised Hemingway and Faulkner for their "willingness to remain in uncertainties, mysteries, and doubts," their talent for seeing "the full force and complexity of their subject matter."[3] And it wasn't only poems and novels that required detailed exegesis. "The problems of national security," wrote Daniel Bell in a characteristic statement, "like those of the national economy, have become so staggeringly complex, that they can no longer be settled by common sense or past experience."[4] If reality was as complex as pluralists said it was, straightforward explanations of events were useless; phenomena had to be interpreted. In *12 Angry Men*, facts don't speak for themselves, and Cobb and friends are blinded by common sense, which assumes that they do. Those jurors who believe that reality is amenable to simple, lay, or amateur interpretation are not only wrong, they're dangerous.

What is at issue in *12 Angry Men* is not only what really happened, but how we find out what really happened, and whom we listen to. The answer, of course, is the corporate liberals themselves. Getting at the truth is a strenuous operation, requiring the intervention of a dispassionate, rational consciousness, which is why the jurors have to be tutored in the language of reality by Fonda. Fonda is an expert who qualifies for his role by virtue of his superior education. The cult of complexity implied that experts—intellectuals, scientists, and technocrats—were the only ones who could understand and therefore run society. Both capitalists and workers, wrote Schlesinger, are trapped in a state of "mutual bewilderment," leaving "the way open for . . . the politician-manager-intellectual types"[5] to step in. Like Fonda, they are well suited to deal with reality because they have the correct ideology, that is, no ideology.

EXTREMISTS REJECT PLURALISM

If Marshall and Fonda represent the center, Cobb and his friends are archetypical versions of what centrists liked to call "extremists." From the vantage point of pluralists, extremists were trolls and goblins who dwelled in darkness outside the center; in short they were totalitarians of the right and left, Fascists and Communists who rejected pluralism, that is, had nothing but contempt for the democratic process. Extremists displayed a "tendency to convert politics into 'moral' issues," wrote Bell, whereupon "political debate moves from specific interest clashes, in which issues can be identified and possibly compromised, to ideologically-tinged conflicts which polarize groups and divide society."[6] Like Barry Goldwater, whose 1964 presidential campaign slogan was "In Your Heart You Know He's Right," they dismissed reason in favor of feeling. They were neurotic "indignants," as Riesman and colleagues called them in *The Lonely Crowd*, troublemakers who got "themselves worked up about political abuses; they have a positive tropism to evidence of race discrimination, police brutality, corporate skullduggery."[7] Extremists, in other words, were radicals, most often of the left, but also of the right, as in *12 Angry*

Men. Left or right, extremists, according to pluralists, were the way they were because they were anxious about their "status." They were insecure because they had risen or fallen too quickly through the ranks of class. In *12 Angry Men*, the status-anxious extremists are either rags-to-riches self-made men like Cobb and Begley or petit-bourgeois losers like Warden.

Although Fonda manages to defeat his extremist opponents in debate, the rules of the jury process, like the rules of pluralism, require that he has to include them in the emerging majority for acquittal. As a good corporate liberal, he believes that a stable society is based on inclusion, not exclusion. So long as groups with competing ideologies subscribed to the ground rules of the center, submitted, as Bell put it, "to the discipline of compromise," to the rules of the game, the center was happy to have them on the team. Therefore, Fonda must conciliate the losers. In one scene, when most of the jurors have risen from the table to turn their backs on Begley, who has made a racist remark, it is Fonda who beckons them back, countering their indignation with a kind word for Begley: "It's always difficult to keep personal prejudice out of a thing like this," he says sympathetically. (A little indignation is a good thing, but too much would threaten to turn the jurors into extremist "indignants" themselves, and interfere with the good-natured give-and-take of pluralist politics.) Fonda finds it easy to forgive Begley, because Begley is essentially sick, not bad. Similarly, near the end, when Cobb sits shattered by the realization that he has failed his son, Fonda welcomes him into the fold by putting a comforting hand on his shoulder. At each other's throats throughout the film, they are now friends. Both have compromised. If Fonda has accepted Cobb into the group, Cobb has swallowed his pride and relinquished his hatred of Fonda. With Cobb on board, finally convinced that he too has a stake in society, the process is completed. When the jurors enter the courtroom at last, Cobb, Begley, and Warden take their places alongside everybody else, join Fonda and Marshall in closing ranks before the world. Their differences are all in the family.

CONSENSUS THROUGH PLURALISM

When Fonda persuades Cobb et al. to join the others, he succeeds in domesticating the extremists, making bad reactionaries into good conservatives. Conservatives were the final ingredient in the fifties political pie. Somewhat to the right of the corporate liberals, they were nevertheless their junior partners. The economic base of conservatism lay in small and medium-sized farms and businesses, along with the new wealth of the Southwest, the area that would later be called the Sunbelt. Their party was the right wing of the Republican Party, the midwestern Old Guard gathered around senators like Dirksen and Knowland, often joined by the right wing of the Democratic Party, the so-called Dixiecrats. Their favorite son and perennial candidate for president was Robert Taft. Conservatives differed from corporate liberals on the details of how things should be run, but in times of crisis, like Cobb and friends, they closed ranks with their corporate-liberal allies, remaining well within the center.

The fruit of Fonda's labors has been the unanimous verdict for acquittal. But the verdict itself feels like an anticlimax. What is important in this film is not that the jury acquitted the defendant but that the decision was unanimous. *12 Angry Men* is more interested in consensus than in justice. Consensus, the shared agreement between corporate liberals and conservatives (however reluctant) on fundamental premises of pluralism, was—outside, perhaps, of the H-bomb—the fifties' most important product. Since *12 Angry Men* endorses consensus, it is a centrist film. And because the consensus is dominated by the corporate liberals and their ideology of pluralism, it is moreover a corporate-liberal or pluralist film.

NOTES

1. David Riesman and Nathan Glazer, "Intellectuals and Discontented Classes," in Daniel Bell, ed., *The Radical Right* (Garden City, N.Y.: Doubleday & Co., Anchor Books, 1964), p. 121.
2. Arthur Schlesinger, Jr., *The Vital Center*, new ed. (London: André Deutsch, 1970), p. 245.
3. Lionel Trilling, *The Liberal Imagination* (Garden City, N.Y.: Doubleday & Co., Anchor Books, 1953), pp. 208, 289.
4. Daniel Bell, "The Dispossessed," in Bell, ed., *The Radical Right*, p. 32.
5. Schlesinger, *Vital Center*, p. 155.
6. Daniel Bell, "Interpretations of American Politics," in Bell, ed., *The Radical Right*, p. 70.
7. David Riesman, Nathan Glazer, and Reuel Denney, *The Lonely Crowd* (Garden City, N.Y.: Doubleday & Co., Anchor Books, 1955), p. 211.

Justice and Democracy Depend on Liberalism and Reason

Frank R. Cunningham

In this article, Frank R. Cunningham explores Sidney Lumet's presentation of the characters in his 1957 film *Twelve Angry Men*. Of particular interest is the manner in which the movie's characters speak to larger issues such as the role of personal responsibility in a democracy, fatherhood and fathering roles in society, and the growth of liberal social values during the 1950s. Cunningham also discusses individual actors' performances in the film, as well as the impressive cinematography of the film. Cunningham is a professor of English at the University of South Dakota, and he has written the book *Sidney Lumet: Film and Literary Vision*.

12 Angry Men (1957), [director Sidney] Lumet's first feature film after seven years of outstanding television productions, stands to this date as one of his most thematically rich and cinematically evocative films. Treating typical Lumet concerns such as the necessity for personal responsibility if democratic processes are to survive, and the tendency for humanity's illusions, guilts, and prejudices to endanger its legal systems, *12 Angry Men* goes beyond the well-intentioned "message picture" to make a remarkable cinematic statement about the nature of the limitations of the American jury system and of the American democratic process itself.

Reginald Rose's screenplay (expanded considerably from his 1954 teleplay) treats the jury deliberation in a murder trial of an eighteen-year-old minority youth accused of the premeditated killing of his father. We do not hear or see any of the trial itself beyond the judge's direction to the jury. Nor do we witness the boy on trial except for one wordless view of him near the beginning of the film. Lumet is uninterested in the legal attack and defense system, in the sometimes pyrotechnic emotional displays by both counsel and witness in American courtrooms. On the contrary, as is so frequent in his films, Lumet here is far more interested in human character, in the nuances of the ways that people make up their minds about things (or think they do), than in the more obvious spectacle of . . . legal melodramas. . . . Almost all of *12 Angry Men* takes place in one small room, a jury room in which sit twelve ordinary men, chosen at random by a human institution that entrusts them with a decision that determines the future of a human life. To all but one of the jurors (all but two of whose names are never known to us), the boy seems clearly guilty as charged on the abundance of circumstantial evidence, and the jury's responsibility seems obvious: they must put a guilty man into the electric chair, despite his youth and the impoverished environment from which he has come and that may well have contributed to his alleged crime. But Juror #8 (Henry Fonda), a soft-spoken architect in his outside life, is not certain that the evidence is sufficiently clear or ample to establish beyond reasonable doubt the boy's guilt. To the surprise of almost all the other eleven jurors—and the anger of a few who feel that the case is so clear that they should be permitted to go about their business—Fonda insists that the case be discussed for a while, that a little of their time is called for before a terminal decision is made regarding a human life.

THE CHARACTERS AND THEIR CONVICTIONS

For the approximately one-and-one-half hours of the film (congruent with the elapsed time of the jury's deliberations), Lumet reveals the processes of thought and feeling of the twelve men as they grapple with the facts of the case, facts that seem to become less clear, more elusive, the more carefully they are reflected upon. Ultimately neither they nor we ever conclusively know the young defendant's guilt or innocence. To Lumet the boy's eventual fate, important as it is, is less significant than the ways in which it affects the minds and sensibilities of the twelve chosen to decide that destiny. Lumet's legendary skill with actors is evident even in this early film, as all the jurors—even those with smaller speaking parts—emerge as recognizable human beings with whose conflicts and weaknesses we can identify. Though a cross-section of middle-class and lower-middle-class New Yorkers, they are individualized by Lumet's unobtrusive yet sharply probing camera eye, sometimes seen from behind Fonda's shoulder as the man of deliberation and reason attempts to argue some jurors out of their prejudices and to persuade others away from their unconsidered conformity or fear. Several of the jurors (John Fiedler, Edward Binns, Martin Balsam, Jack Klugman) are "average" men, some more intelligent and reflective than others, who wish justice to be done. Yet their natural tendency to follow others leads them often to defer to the ill-considered judgments of the impatient and careless (Jack Warden, Robert Webber), the intemperate (Ed Begley), or the deeply conflicted (Lee J. Cobb). Pivotal to the decisions and conflicts of these less self-realized jurors is the juror played by E.G. Marshall, whose greater insight and intelligence sometimes is as endangered by his own preconceptions and illusions as by the dogmatism and prejudice of those more fearful and dependent than himself. An "expertly fashioned" actor's picture, *12 Angry Men* reveals "individuals exposed as being ridden by fears . . . and an aversion to analytical thinking."[1]

At a sociological level, clearly Lumet's film reflects strong concern with the constituent parts of a living democracy, as the wiser and more emotionally stable jurors must responsibly lead those men with less self-awareness and self-knowledge than they, if democracy is to have any chance to work fairly and justly. Though the film contains little doctrinaire preaching on the subject of democracy, the audience is led to respond favorably to those jurors—Fonda, Joseph Sweeney, George Voskovec—for whom reason and the liberal vision of the world and of humankind are paramount. Nowhere is Rose's screenplay more subtly eloquent than in the scene in which Voskovec, an East European immigrant watchmaker now proud of his American citizenship, berates Warden, the successful marmalade salesman, for casting a crucial vote thoughtlessly, in simple indifference and haste, so that he can get to his baseball game on time. Whenever Voskovec speaks of democracy, he does so simply, out of the harsh experience of a man who has seen another political system up close and has found it wanting. He insists that if people are to govern themselves and their social relationships fairly and reasonably, then they must be guided by principle. As he forces Warden for the first time to state his convictions for casting his vote, to ask questions of himself, Lumet frames Voskovec coming toward Warden's seat in an extremely tight close-up, but with the camera tilted only slightly up at the watchmaker, as if to minimize the European's "heroism" and to make him less important than the convictions for which he stands. The subtlety of this low-angle shot in an emotionally heightened scene underscores visually the fact that though Voskovec may regard Warden with contempt, he does not consider himself—nor does Lumet consider him— intrinsically superior to the all-American baseball fan.

THE JUSTICE SYSTEM IN A LIBERAL DEMOCRACY

Earlier in the film, as a few of the jurors take a break from the sometimes angry debate, Lumet's meditative camera follows Fonda and Binns to the washroom, where Binns, an earnest working man who honestly disagrees with Fonda, states his conviction of the boy's guilt. After a critical comment about the irrationality and unfairness of some of the jurors who support his own position, Binns says, "I'm not used to supposin', I'm just a workin' man, my boss does all the supposin'." Yet he calls Fonda back as Fonda is about to return to his seat in the jury room: "But supposin' you do talk us all out of this and the kid really did knife his father?" The well-intentioned juror misses the point, of course, that the jury system exists at least as much to protect the innocent as to convict the guilty. Holding Binns in steady midshot during this brief scene, Lumet suggests more, however, than the intellectual vacuity of this decent man; he emphasizes the fact that those who do not exercise their imaginative faculty, who do not "suppose," make weak cogs in a social system based supposedly upon the imaginative use of reason. That this sequence takes place in the most mundane location of the film underscores the basic importance of the theme of democracy in *12 Angry Men;* here its "hero" shows a penchant for fastidious cleanliness. It is not the character of Juror #8 that Lumet celebrates in the film, but rather the man's reasoned use of principle.

Lumet visually enhances his concern with the workings of the liberal democratic system early in the film, when, having walked into the barren, sultry jury room, Warden and Binns manage, with a difficulty emblematic of the film's action, to raise the window together. Moments later, Robert Webber, a slogan-spouting advertising executive in private

JUROR #8 IS THE PERFECT HERO FOR THE EDUCATED, LIBERAL VIEWER

Movie critic Pauline Kael asserts that Twelve Angry Men *will be most appreciated by viewers who identify with the liberal hero standing up for a minority victim.*

The social worker-at-heart finds true reassurance when the modern-designed movie also has modern design built into the theme: a movie like *Twelve Angry Men.* Ask an educated American what he thought of *Twelve Angry Men* and more likely than not he will reply, "That movie made some good points" or "It got some important ideas across." His assumption is that it carried these ideas, which also happen to be his ideas, to the masses. Actually, it didn't: this tense, ingenious juryroom melodrama was a flop with the mass audience, a success only at revivals in art houses.

The social psychology of *Twelve Angry Men* is perfectly attuned to the educated audience. The hero, Henry Fonda—the one against the eleven—is lean, intelligent, gentle but strong, this liberal, fair-minded architect is *their* hero. And the boy on trial is their dream of a victim: he is of some unspecified minority, he is a slum product who never had a chance, and, to clinch the case, his father didn't love him. It isn't often that professional people can see themselves on the screen as the hero—in this case the Lincolnesque architect of the future—and how they love it! They are so delighted to see a movie that demonstrates a proposition they have already accepted that they cite *Twelve Angry Men* . . . as evidence that American movies are really growing up.

Pauline Kael, *I Lost It at the Movies*, 1965.

life and one of the least sympathetic of the jurors, happens on the democratic idea that the eleven jurors convinced of the defendant's guilt present their reasons in turn, in order to attempt to convince Fonda of the rightness of a guilty verdict. But the four-minute, wordless opening sequence of the film most impressively and succinctly represents the principles of reason and liberalism that *12 Angry Men* upholds. After an establishing shot of the city courthouse, Lumet's camera tilts very slowly upward toward the building's four framing pillars; a huge lamp hangs down from the exact center of the frame, at the top of which is seen a motto carved in stone: "Administration of Justice is the Firmest Pillar of Good Government." Against the background sound of city traffic noise, Lumet cuts to an equally slow downward tilt from inside the courthouse, from a large chandelier at ceiling level down to the center cupola, again precisely framed between four inner pillars. Pausing at the level of the second landing, the camera observes five people passing slowly near one another from several directions and converging at a point directly beneath the hanging chandelier. Their carefully orchestrated passage, reminiscent of the balletlike passing sequence in [Orson] Welles's *Magnificent Ambersons,* offers a symmetrical arrangement that parallels the carefully framed backdrop against which they move. By his formal composition and intrashot montage, Lumet suggests a tone of almost classical stateliness and rationality for the forthcoming action. The extraordinarily leisurely camera movements, featuring but one cut in almost four minutes and ending in a slow tracking shot to the outside of the courtroom where the boy's trial is being conducted, imply that the course of human justice is glacially slow and that only the classical values of ordered, reasoned, meditative inquiry will possibly defeat the irrational prejudice that we are soon to see dominating the jury room. Typically, Lumet's cinematic technique does not call attention to itself here, but its union with the film's thematic and moral meaning reminds the film viewer that the purpose of technique in any art form is less for spectacle than for serving the thematic values of the work of art itself. Rarely a pretentious, self-conscious artist, Lumet here reveals, quite early in his directorial career, that his central aesthetic interests lie in joining as closely as possible artistic content and form into a mutually integrative web of meaning.

THE SIGNIFICANCE OF PERSONAL RESPONSIBILITY

Part of the subtext of that meaning throughout *12 Angry Men* is the significance of personal responsibility if a just, civilized order is to continue and flourish. A central concern in many of Lumet's films . . . —the responsibility of the individual—is especially pertinent in *12 Angry Men* in the characterizations of Fonda, Voskovec, Sweeney, and Balsam. Fonda risks censure and ridicule by all his peers on the jury for his initial stand: "Well, I guess we talk. . . . It's not easy to raise my hand and send a boy off to die without talking about it first." Throughout the first half of the film, he continues to risk the sneering disapproval of Warden and Begley and even the im-

plied violence of Cobb, whom he goads and satirizes on occasion to try to show him his own potential for violence that
subconsciously prejudices him against the youthful defendant. Fonda occasionally pontificates on personal responsibility (one of the film's few aesthetic weaknesses), but a more
subtly crucial sequence involving the theme concerns Martin
Balsam, the jury foreman. Trying to organize the proceedings, he is called "a kid" by Begley. When he challenges Begley, saying that someone has to chair the jury, and asks him
to take the first chair, Begley promptly backs away from assuming the responsibility. When Webber, trying to smooth
over the rift, denies the importance altogether of the principle of jury leadership, Lumet cuts to Balsam seated twisted in
his foreman's chair, in extreme close-up right profile, with
Warden's offscreen, unintentionally ironic condolence, "You
stay in there and pitch," emphasizing Balsam's feelings of
powerlessness and disgust. After Fonda attempts to salvage
something of his pride and of the group's order, Balsam is
again shown, face turned away from the jury table, saying, "I
don't care *what* you do," resignedly chewing his nails.

Shortly after this, Fonda gambles on a second ballot—this
one secret—and Sweeney, the oldest member of the jury by
many years, changes his vote. As Lumet cuts down-angle at
him to stress his function and not any sense of self-
importance, Sweeney speculates about chance and possibility and defends Fonda's motives for standing heretofore
alone against the group. But as he speaks, Warden insults
the old man by leaving the table for the men's room; as
Sweeney remonstrates against this indignity, Fonda says
softly, "He can't hear you, he never will." Here Lumet inter-
weaves, as he does often in the film, a motif of fathering that
becomes an important visual correlative to the theme of the
necessity for personal responsibility in an increasingly de-
personalized, bureaucratized world. The boy is on trial for
the primal crime, the murder of the father, the crime that
Freud posits as underlying most feelings of guilt and so
much human misery. Throughout his attempt to induce
fairness and reason among the jurors weighing this alleged
crime, Fonda—and to a lesser extent Sweeney, Voskovec,
and Marshall—become fathers to the other jurors, disclos-
ing to some of them to some degree, at least, the sources of
their irrational responses to the issues in the trial. Lumet, always sensitive to psychoanalytic motifs in his films, en-

hances the dramatic and visual power of *12 Angry Men* through the use of these motifs.

FATHER IMAGES

Our first image of fathering (aside from a brief glimpse of a man carrying a child in the silent four-minute sequence that opens the film) is hardly reassuring: Lumet cuts from the opening sequence to a close-up of a bored-looking judge instructing the jury on the law of premeditation in murder. As the judge concludes his comments, saying, "You're faced with a grave responsibility, thank you, gentlemen," his right hand props up his cheek as with his left he reaches for a glass of water. We sense that, although he is languidly adhering to the forms of the law, he is ignoring its spirit and thus setting a poor example for at least some members of the jury. (Lumet at this point pans slowly over the jury panel for the first time: Warden and Cobb seem not to pay any attention to what the judge says.) As the jurors leave, Lumet stages one of his memorable sequences in the film: shot from over the right shoulder of the defendant (John Savoca), we see the twelve jurors file out toward the jury room. Some look back at the boy nervously, but Webber just flips his lapels to cool off while idly glancing at the youth, his mind obviously made up, his guilty vote cast before he reaches the jury room. Lumet then cuts to an extreme close-up of the defendant's face, an unforgettable image that Lumet holds for twenty seconds. He is a boy, looking younger than his eighteen years. He is perhaps Mexican or Puerto Rican but is quite light-skinned (soon after this shot, the bigot Begley will rant that it is not surprising that "these kids" murder their fathers). Most memorable are the boy's eyes. They stare out at the courtroom, not angrily, but passively, whether all-knowing or uncomprehending we never know. For the final seconds of this shot, Lumet gradually superimposes the defendant's face over the empty jury room where his judges will decide his fate. As the superimposition occurs, his eyes are sharply downcast; the entire shot is from a slightly high angle as if to accentuate his vulnerability at the hands of these fathers.

As the men mill about waiting to convene, Binns approaches the men's room door to summon Sweeney, then helps him into his chair, treating the elder with the respect that he will show him throughout the film. Sweeney does not fulfill the father role psychologically until Fonda's courage and determination—which initially place Fonda in the role of father to Sweeney—enable the older man to assume a leadership role when he changes his vote to not guilty. Particularly interesting is Lumet's handling of the relationship between the Fonda-Sweeney axis and Juror #3, Lee J. Cobb. Cobb, who has driven his own son from him because of his barely suppressed violence many years before, is the juror most in need of fathering. He is also the most irresponsible, since he seems unable to exercise rational judgment in dealing with an issue that calls up dimly realized personal associations for him that are highly charged with subliminal energy. Cobb runs a messenger service, and early in the film he hands his card to businessman Marshall, saying that he "started with nothing." His occasional turning to Marshall for reassurance, particularly when his emotional gaps have been exposed by Fonda or Sweeney, suggests that Cobb himself has experienced an unfortunate relationship with his own father that has soured him to the extent that he has become dictatorial and unforgiving in most of his human relationships.

One of the subtlest camera movements in the film occurs as Marshall gives his opening arguments against Fonda. Cobb, having finished his statement to the group (which concerned the old man who testified that he lived in the room beneath the scene of the crime and heard everything), walks slowly around the table toward the slowly backward-tracking camera and toward the water cooler, looking intently at a small photograph—we learn later that it is a picture of his estranged son. Marshall's voice offscreen says that he feels it is not the jury's business to go into the reasons why the defendant "grew up the way he did." At these words, Cobb, now in extreme close-up, looks up sharply from his son's picture. Though he says nothing and the camera almost immediately shifts to another juror, Lumet swiftly etches the first touching of the film's rawest nerve. Moments later, as Marshall discusses the exhibit murder weapon—a switchblade stiletto—the camera tracks slowly, following Marshall back to his seat at the table. Just at the instant when Marshall recounts that the defendant allegedly had another fight with his father, Cobb alone of the other jurors is visible in deepest frame behind Marshall.

During the episode in which Fonda attempts to disprove

the testimony of the old man who said he heard the crime committed in the room above his, Sweeney movingly attests to the old witness's possible motive for testifying, leaving unspoken his own fears of his existence as a forgotten, unknown old man. As Cobb berates Sweeney for his sympathy to the old witness, Lumet cuts to Sweeney twice in reaction shots that key Binns's defense of Sweeney, whom Binns is beginning to appreciate for enlightening him. Binns threatens Cobb, reminding him that he "ought to treat an old man with respect." Sweeney continues with an argument that gets at the heart of why Cobb and the other jurors who possess minimal self-understanding have such difficulty in acting responsibly: he argues that the old witness, because of his loneliness, his need for a moment in the sun, might have come to believe his own story. Lumet for the first time treats a theme he returns to again and again in his films: human beings' propensity to delude themselves, to become so immured in their illusions that they come to be bound by them, even to the extent that they lack awareness of their self-induced imprisonment.

In the latter half of the film, Cobb becomes increasingly isolated from the rest of the jurors because of such psychological unawareness. After Fonda goads Cobb into rushing at him in an attempt to show Cobb how close to the surface are his impulses, Lumet isolates Cobb from the group so completely that he is out of the frame, as the rest stare into a seemingly nonexistent plane of space. Moments later, as Cobb tries to regain lost prestige with the group by giving a demonstration of how the angle of the knife's descent could have been down and in even allowing for a seven-inch height difference between the murdered father and the smaller son, he unwittingly becomes son to Fonda's father. In one of the film's tensest moments, Cobb approaches the camera (Fonda's point of view), slowly raises the knife from a stooped posture, then quickly starts his hand downward. Lumet switches to a two[-person] shot, and Cobb slowly drops the knife into Fonda's breast pocket. While seemingly he has gained status and relieved his emotional blocks by this thought-murder of the father, Lumet's visual irony catches Cobb reducing his stature considerably below that of Fonda, metaphorically as well as physically. Cobb's performance here as throughout is superb; his voice breaks as he says, "Nobody's hurt . . . down and in, down and in." But

Lumet holds the two-shot long enough for the calm Fonda to repeat his words, thus emphasizing Fonda's own superior role in the tortuous process of teaching Cobb self-awareness and, with it, social responsibility.

INDIVIDUAL PERFORMANCES ARE SUPERIOR

Lumet elicits superior performances from all the members of his cast, both individually and as an ensemble. Balsam speaks movingly of the joy he gains from his high school coaching job, Klugman of his nurture in the city's ghettos. Lumet's skill and care in extensive rehearsals produces a gem by Voskovec. When Webber patronizes Voskovec by his suggestion that the finest watchmakers come from his part of Europe, Voskovec's courtly, barely discernible little bow perfectly ironizes the ad man's unconscious penchant for consistently adopting the jargon and hypocrisy he publicly scorns. Webber's performance enhances the motif of the imprisoning power of self-delusion; at the start of the jury's deliberations, he adjusts his collar and tie carefully, as if he thinks he is at a meeting of account executives. This self-proclaimed liberal amuses himself during his debate with games of tic-tac-toe and polishing his sales pitch for his company's newest breakfast cereal; his unconscious and cheapened liberalism is the focus of Lumet's most sustained visual satire in the film.

E.G. Marshall's performance is one of the film's most compelling and restrained. The enlightened, rational, responsible conservative is Fonda's most formidable adversary, for in him Fonda does not oppose undue prejudice or a careless mind. Juror #4 is a highly educated, judicious, and cultured stockbroker; he is convinced of the boy's guilt primarily because the boy cannot remember what he did after his father allegedly struck him twice on the night of the murder and because of the testimony of a woman who said she saw the killing through the windows of a passing elevated train from across the street. In another of Lumet's superior visual presentations in *12 Angry Men*, Marshall . . . wearing his coat and tie through the oppressive summer heat even when a sudden storm forces the closing of the windows, is challenged by Fonda to remember his own movements of the last four evenings. Although Marshall calmly replies to Fonda's questioning that even under great stress he could remember exactly what he was doing at any recent time during his past (and thus he implies that the boy from an underprivileged class should be able to remember, too, if he were innocent), Fonda finds details that Marshall cannot recall, albeit the stockbroker's life is a comfortable one, with little stress.

LEARNING EXPERIENCES LEAD TO
SELF-KNOWLEDGE AND RESPONSIBILITY

The sequence begins with a cut to Fonda over Marshall's right shoulder—a frame that Lumet uses often in the film to accentuate the cramped existential space people sometimes have for the working-out of problems and dilemmas. Then Lumet cuts down to Marshall over Fonda's left knee and elbow, a shot that seems to trap Marshall by further reducing the space in which he must think and try to remember. As he struggles to recall the title of a movie he saw a few evenings back when he was completely relaxed, Lumet frames Marshall against the window upon which the rain beats. During cuts between the two men, the wooden sill below the window in deep rear frame passes behind Marshall just at his neck, suggesting the distancing of his cognitive faculties from his abilities to empathize with the traumatic emotional condition of a boy who has been seriously underprivileged since early childhood. Fonda, however, is completely framed by a door far behind him, suggesting his greater emotional spaciousness and psychological integration. Further, Lumet gradually increases the sound of the rain driving against the window during his cuts to Marshall and the background windowsill in this sequence, as Marshall learns from the wiser juror something of the difficulty—particularly for the less-privileged classes—of containing life's mystery, its constantly changing impressions, into comforting fixities. As Marshall makes these discoveries, Lumet's final extreme close-up reveals a single bead of sweat forming on his forehead.

At other points in the film Lumet uses the jury room window and its connotations of psychological spaciousness as a backdrop for other small learning experiences in the jurors' paths to greater self-knowledge and responsibility. Early in the film Webber comments to Fonda as both stand at the window that, even though he has lived in New York all his life, he never realized the Woolworth Building was exactly there. When Begley, the bigoted garage owner, after demeaning Balsam for trying to conduct the jury's discussions according to principles of order, gains a glimmering of awareness that he fears the responsibility of acting as foreman, Lumet positions him at the window. Fonda gazes out the window as he gambles on a second, secret ballot, hoping to find at least one ally in his fight for the boy's life. Just as the thunderstorm breaks late in the film, Balsam and Fonda close the windows, and Balsam gives his moving speech about the joys he gains from his coaching work.

CAMERA WORK ENHANCES THE MOOD

Director of photography Boris Kaufman, one of the most distinguished cinematographers in black and white and Lumet's most frequent cinematographer through the middle sixties, praised Lumet's "fine and sensitive . . . feel for camera-work" in an article dealing with the great difficulties of making the film dynamic given such a small working space. (Other than the opening sequence, and the final sequence as the jurors leave the jury room, the entire film takes place on one set—the cramped, barely furnished jury room, "a room no larger than an average hotel room.") Lumet and Kaufman decided to take advantage of the cramped space by making the sense of confinement an integral part of the visual mood. As the film's tensions mount, Lumet changes lenses to give the effect of crowding at the table over which the jurors argue. The lighting gradually grows darker as the thunderstorm approaches and as issues and men reach a breaking point. During the long take as the men first enter the jury room—to that point, the longest single continuous take in Kaufman's career—Lumet introduces the psychological characteristics of the jurors as they mill about the room and bump into one another. Revealing gestures (Fonda's meditative tapping of his fingers as he stands at the window) and casual comments (the frustrated Begley's cynical comments about the defendant, Warden's clichéd talk about baseball) that seem irrelevant to the case presage the inner nature of the combatants, twelve men, said Boris Kaufman, "whose backgrounds, attitudes, problems, and reasons behind their decisions had to be shown photographically as well as in the dialogue."[2]

Critics such as Andrew Sarris have often criticized Lumet for literary "pretentiousness" yet he has steadfastly refused to consider film as a wordless medium, while at the same time adhering to the principle that, as Kaufman has said, in "good cinematography the camera should never distract the audience from the basic theme and never move without justification."[3] In a *New York Times* interview, Lumet spoke with typical brio about his distaste for the self-consciously "tricky" film. He said that he vetoed having a glass top on the jury table to allow trick camera shots and added: "Some people have suggested that the picture needs jazzing up. For instance, somebody had the idea that we should explain that all the regular jury rooms are occupied and have this in the basement, where we could show the exposed pipes and maybe the furnace in order to provide pictorial contrast. But we threw the idea out." Speaking to the actors during rehearsal, Lumet commented: "There's going to be no artificiality in this. You are going to be the whole picture. This is not a tract. This is not a pro-jury or anti-jury thing. It's . . . about human behavior. No glass table tops. No basement room. Just you and the fullness of your behavior."[4]

As this remark indicates, Lumet's union of cinematic technique with literary and thematic moral meaning precisely defines his directorial significance. Lumet may not always move the camera in ways that call immediate attention to his technique (thus his low ranking in Sarris's 1968 hierarchies), yet his frame is rarely static but usually full, busy with life's detail and flow. Though the camera work is seldom spectacular, its controlled movement is subtle and filled with the movement of human event. Some critics habitually and impressionistically criticize Lumet for weak visuals and overdependence on dialogue and for an insufficiently personal vision. Lumet creates all his own frames and shots, and he has done so since the beginning of his directorial career.

The greater depth of characterization and theme in Lumet's finished film when compared with both [the television and film] versions of Reginald Rose's play indicates Lumet's originality.[5] For instance, Lumet represents the character of Juror #9 (Joseph Sweeney) as stronger and more emotionally durable than Rose's original characterization of him as "long since defeated by life and now merely waiting to die." As directed by Lumet, the foreman (Martin Balsam) is far more sensitive and aware of ambiguities than is indicated by Rose's original depiction of him as "impressed with the authority he has . . . petty . . . dogged." Lumet's direction of Cobb (Juror #3) brings out in full the messenger service owner's latent sadism barely hinted at in the play. The memorable shot of the defendant's face in extreme close-up for twenty seconds has no correlative in Rose's play; likewise, Lumet's brilliant early visual presentation of the hall of justice is absent in the play except for a bare reference to the play's judicial setting in the expanded version.[6] Most crucial, however, is the deletion in the film of the sentimentality that now and then surfaces in the play. Early in the action when Sweeney remonstrates against Begley's bigotry, Lumet omits reference to this flowery passage: "Somehow his [Fonda's] touch and his gentle expression calm the old man. He draws a deep breath and relaxes." Gone as well in the film is Rose's unnecessarily sensational episode in which Juror #3 advances upon Juror #8 at the end of the play with the exhibit knife as if to stab him, and Juror #8 grabs the knife. Lumet also mercifully omits the closing close-up of "a slip of crumpled paper on which are scribbled the words 'not guilty.'" Indeed, even the longer version contains but three references to any sort of camera movement or technique.

LUMET'S PERSISTENT LIBERALISM

12 Angry Men also reflects a strain of persistent liberalism in Lumet that is out of fashion among many of today's academic intellectuals and critical writers. Lumet has never favored radical-chic style or content in his films, and his strong penchant for meditative psychoanalytic themes has also not endeared him to the film critics' establishment. Nowhere does the film defer to, for example, Webber's shallow liberal view that the American judicial system is a perfect institution. Lumet's films are much like the basic themes in this film: the evidence is to be respected; theory is less trustworthy than the particularity of each instance of reality as the characters perceive it. Lumet refuses to make films that as a group easily fall into categories. Of course, facile categories and theories make headlines, and so the Godards [French director Jean-Luc Godard] gain more fame than the Frankenheimers [American director John Frankenheimer], even though work without such theoretical embellishment may possess the greater excellence. Given Lumet's strong commitment that the technique must suit the theme of the particular work of art, his cinematic style has received much less attention than it deserves, and certain recurrent

motifs and themes throughout the oeuvre have been un-
justly ignored.

But although Lumet is an "old-fashioned" liberal committed to looking at themes of personal responsibility and to
looking at each situation on its own terms, he refuses to give
his audience what some liberals did in the 1950s: the comforting illusion that there are relatively easy answers to
complex questions. (See the ambiguities and unresolved situations at the end of *Prince of the City,* Lumet's 1981 crime
film, as we are moved both to applause for and hostility toward the police informer played by Treat Williams.) All
Lumet offers us in *12 Angry Men* is that, given the prepon-
derance of irrationality in this society in the 1950s (as perhaps best represented by Warden and Begley), the liberal
and humane solution represented by Fonda is just possible
on a limited basis, case by case. As in [Ralph Waldo] Emerson's time, democracy is still an individual, personal concern with no easy answers, just the necessity of hard work
and patience to combat the chicanery and ignorance all
about us. This great theme—distinguishing Lumet's work
from *12 Angry Men* and *Fail Safe* through *Serpico, Prince of
the City,* and *Running on Empty*—is, of course, no more
fashionable in the age of Godard than it was in the day of
Emerson. As the *Time* review notes, "The law is no better
than the people who enforce it, and . . . the people who enforce it are all too human."[7]

Perhaps Lumet's fine conjoining of theme and visual technique is most evident in the film's final sequence, as Cobb
caps his wrenching performance by admitting his frustration
and sorrow over his past treatment of his son, tearing up the
boy's picture and sobbing out the final "not guilty" that will
clear the defendant on the existence of a reasonable doubt of
his guilt. Lumet shows Cobb against the window of reality, of
flux and change, as he cries out his symbolic confession. After Fonda helps Cobb put on his coat as the jurors get ready
to leave, Lumet shows the anonymous jurors—with the significant exceptions of the film's prime fathers, Fonda and
Sweeney, who momentarily introduce themselves—slowly
coming down the steps beneath the columns seen in the
opening sequence and one by one going their own ways,
some across the street into a park opposite the courthouse.
Cobb, the last one down the steps, walks very slowly, glancing at Fonda, who disappears into frame right. Cobb is boxed

in by the two rows of stair railings in frame left, as if made partially aware by the events of the trial that he has far to go to reach the serene spaciousness of the park across the street into which the others have blended.

FOOTNOTES

1. A.H. Weiler, *New York Times,* April 21, 1957, sec. 2, p. 1.
2. Boris Kaufman, "Filming *12 Angry Men* on a Single Set," *American Cinematographer* 37 (Dec. 1956): 724–25.
3. See Andrew Sarris's impressionistic account of Lumet's career in *The American Cinema: Directors and Directions, 1929–1968* (New York: Dutton, 1968), 198; Kaufman, "Filming *Twelve Angry Men,*" 725.
4. Don Ross, "A Dozen Happy Actors Become 'Twelve Angry Men,'" *New York Times,* July 15, 1956, sec. 4, p. 3.
5. Reginald Rose, "Twelve Angry Men," in *Six Television Plays* (New York: Simon and Schuster, 1956). Quotations from Rose's play are cited in the text.
6. In William I. Kaufman, ed., *Great Television Plays* (New York: Dell, 1969).
7. *Time,* April 29, 1957, p. 96.

Twelve Angry Men Produces Critical Thinking About the Jury System

Henry F. Nardone

In the following article, Henry F. Nardone, a professor of philosophy at King's College in Wilkes-Barre, Pennsylvania, discusses several valuable points of study for the 1957 film version of *Twelve Angry Men*. First, he considers the playwright's purposes in the story, specifically discussing how it is a commentary on the entire jury system. Second, he reviews the evidence against the defendant in the story. Finally, he analyzes the major character traits and contributions of the individual jurors.

The jury system is widely considered one of the most fundamental of our democratic institutions, as traditional in Anglo-Saxon culture as is the common law itself. In the film *12 Angry Men*, Juryman #11, an immigrant, admonishes his fellow citizens that they are privileged to be "notified" that they are to serve as jurors and pass judgment on the fate of a stranger. Such a privilege, he notes to his fellow jury persons is theirs not because of their status, educational background, or familial affiliations, but simply because of their citizenship.

EXAMINING THE JURY SYSTEM

In a sense then, the defendant in this film is not only the young man accused of killing his father but the jury itself, and not just this jury but the entire jury system. Reginald Rose, the co-producer (along with Henry Fonda) of the film (released in 1957) and script writer for the 1954 CBS *Studio One* television show on which the film is based, clearly un-

Excerpted from "Using the Film *Twelve Angry Men* to Teach Critical Thinking," by Henry F. Nardone, in *Proceedings of the Third International Conference on Argumentation*, edited by H. Eemeren, R. Grootenndorst, A. Blair, and C. Willards (Netherlands: International Centre for the Study of Argumentation, 1995). Reprinted by permission of Henry F. Nardone.

derstands the privilege and importance of jurors in a democratic system. In the film Rose further democratizes the jury member's role by omitting names for his jurors. Numbered but not named, they comprise a cross-section of American society; that their value for Rose is as social representatives rather than as individuals is also clear from the brief character descriptions that open his script. Nevertheless, Rose's own cultural and historical context still reveals itself: the jury is composed of 12 angry *men,* women are not represented except for one female eye-witness who is only referred to but not present; also when ethnic prejudice is expressed, as in the case of Juror #10, the Garage Owner, it is more blatant than is the case in our times.

The jury's inability to recognize that the evidence against the defendant is in some ways ambiguous, capable of generating a reasonable doubt, is perhaps, the moral of the story. They are ready, all except Juror #8, to wrap up the case, send the boy to the chair, and then go home and forget it. Their failure is not so much a function of the evidence but of the prejudices and secret hostilities that each juror carries within him. In short, it is a function of the psychological flaws of the twelve human beings, who are assembled from a random venire list to pass judgment on a stranger.

Some film reviewers speculated that *12 Angry Men* is best interpreted as an intentional attack on the jury system, but most see it as a tribute to this system, as reinforcing the notion that a jury of one's peers is one of the best institutions for discovering truth and allocating justice in human affairs. While perhaps not intended as an attack on the jury system, the film nevertheless questions the ultimate fairness and reliability of such a system. As we know, the Constitution guarantees everyone a fair trial by one's peers. The defendant is an uneducated, teenage Puerto Rican slum dweller. The "peers" who comprise his jury are white, generally middle-aged, middle-classed males. Nevertheless, these men have chosen to decide whether he lives or dies even though most seem obviously unable to empathize with his circumstances.

The script suggests that these men, in addition to being socially, culturally, and racially divergent, are more importantly, indifferent. As in Rose's previous work, the film deals with social injustice—the boy on trial is the victim of a brutal father and a sordid environment. And again as in his previous work, the film demonstrates Rose's thesis that an innocent person may be trapped in a net of circumstantial evidence and that people should suspend their judgment until offered clear proof of guilt beyond a reasonable doubt.

The subject of *12 Angry Men,* a murder, associates it with crime movies. But it is not a typical detective movie, one usually involving a thrilling and dangerous search for a killer. *12 Angry Men* is not a thriller in this sense of the term but a realistic attempt to examine the working of a social institution designed specifically to elicit truth. Its vitality and usefulness for teaching critical thinking stem from its demonstration that truth is rarely of the factual kind perceived directly without an inductive or deductive struggle. In a real situation, it often happens that we encounter several versions of the truth, or what several different people will argue should be accepted as the truth.

This, of course, makes the determination of justice an extremely complex, often unsatisfactory, matter. In fact, in *12 Angry Men,* the final verdict is not that the defendant is innocent (he could have killed his father) but only that the evidence, after closer examination, does not allow for a verdict of guilty beyond a reasonable doubt. Eleven of the jurors move from an initial position of certainty about their verdict to a true appreciation of what it means to speak of a "reasonable doubt," as their certainties dissolve in the reexamination of the "facts." The film is practically a primer in the definition and clarification of those important words, "a reasonable doubt." The entire action is concerned with establishing it.

THE INITIAL EVIDENCE POINTS TO THE DEFENDANT'S GUILT

Cinematically the film effectively captures the claustrophobic atmosphere of the jury room. The characters complain incessantly about the heat, the humidity and the stifling lack of air. Even before the deliberations begin Juror #7 laments to his fellow jurors that "this is going to be the hottest day of the year." The prospect of reexamining the evidence in these circumstances makes the jury members grumble and mutter as they take on a grim, horribly persecuted attitude. They all seem to be thinking to themselves the thought "Eight million people in New York and they have to call me." The tension and irritation generated by the proceedings further help to create an uncomfortable environment. The room becomes a pressure-cooker ready to burst from the pent up energies inside. As a consequence, given these elements as well as the excellent acting and photography, reviewing the film is a very powerful and emotional experience.

The defendant is accused of killing his father with a switch-blade knife after a quarrel and the evidence for this accusation is based on the following pieces of evidence:

(1) Testimony of the Old Man: An old man who lives in the apartment just below where the killing took place claims to have heard the accused son yell, "I'm going to kill you" and then a second later heard the father's body hit the floor above his ceiling. The same old man claims, after walking to his apartment's door, to have seen the boy escaping down the stairs after the crime was committed.

(2) Testimony of the Middle-aged Woman: A middle-aged woman claims she saw the accused kill his father from across the street through the windows of the last two cars of a passing elevated ("el") train.

(3) Weapon: The murder weapon used to kill the father was allegedly unique, "one of a kind," so testified the shop-keeper who sold the switchblade knife to the defendant. As a part of his alibi, the defendant claims to have lost it through a hole in his pocket on the way home from the movies.

(4) Weak Alibi: The accused has a weak alibi: he claims he was at the movies when his father was killed but he could not remember the names of the films or who played in them when interrogated by the police. Furthermore, there was no one who saw him leave his apartment for the movies nor would anyone testify that they saw the boy at the theater.

(5) Motive: It is alleged that the boy had a motive for killing his father. Prior to the murder, just a few hours before it occurred, neighbors heard the father and son quarreling and they claimed the boy was either punched or slapped by his father.

(6) Criminal Record: The boy had a history and prior record of crime. He had been involved in several knife fights, struck one of his teachers, and was once arrested for car theft. While this is, of course, not evidence of guilt, it is at least strongly consistent with guilt. He seems to be the kind of boy who was capable of such a crime.

Shortly after the jury members convene these pieces of evidence are reexamined. After the preliminary ballot, a secret ballot and then three more calls for a formal vote, the jury members slowly move towards a reversal of their original positions. Each member changes his view, almost on an individual basis, as each piece of evidence is undermined or as he becomes individually frustrated by the lack of unanimity. Under the guidance primarily of Juror #8, the jurors finally see that they are unable to come up with an unequivocal basis for guilt of the defendant beyond a reasonable doubt.

CHARACTER TRAITS AND CONTRIBUTIONS OF INDIVIDUAL JURORS

Juror #1 (High-School Coach played by Martin Balsam): He is a likable "good Joe," an average guy who is somewhat unsure of himself, but, as foreman is impressed with his authority. As a consequence, he handles the jury proceedings somewhat formally. While he makes no specific contribution to a critical analysis of the evidence presented, he should be credited with recognizing and implementing the suggestion, made by Juror #12 (the ad man), that they go around the table once and those who voted for guilty on the preliminary ballot give their reasons. He keeps the deliberations on track, for the most part, and holds tempers in check through several heated outbreaks. After receiving some criticism he threatens to quit as foreman, but being encouraged to continue, he decides to stay at the post. Even still, he remains offended by any criticism, pouts after he receives it, and effectively drops out of any further active contribution to the deliberations.

Juror #2 (Bank Clerk played by John Fiedler): He is a meek, hesitant introvert who finds it difficult to assert himself but who gets in some shots at his antagonizing fellow jurors. He commits the appeal to ignorance fallacy: when first asked to defend his opinion regarding the defendant's guilt, he replies, "Nobody proved otherwise." Juror #8 quickly responds that the defendant should be presumed innocent and has no obligation to prove anything. In the course of the film Juror #2 does show some independent thinking, however: he catches Juror #3 in an inconsistency, "You said we could throw out all the other evidence." He also questions whether the defendant could have made a downward stab into his father, given the fact that his father was seven inches taller.

Juror #3 (Head of Messenger Service played by Lee J. Cobb): He is a very strong, forceful, opinionated man, easily stirred to outbursts of emotion, especially, anger, which he regrets soon afterward. "You work your heart out," he says several times, apparently addressed to his unappreciative family, especially his son with whom he holds an unresolved conflict and consequent anger that seems unconsciously projected upon the defendant. It is this same anger that he holds towards his son that he projects unconsciously on the entire younger generation, and in doing so commits the fallacy of hasty generalization.

While he complains that the younger generation no longer treats their elders with respect, ironically, he shows little respect for his elder, Juror #9. Ironically again, he is the first to note the eye-witness testimony of the old man who lived below the apartment where the murder took place, and then later in the deliberations, he says, inconsistently, "he was an old man how could he correctly remember anything?"

He is not an inherently mean or malicious man, but he has treated his son badly in the past and displays a streak of sadism when he volunteers to be one of the executioners for the defendant. In his own mind he thinks he uses pure logic and prides himself when he raises what he thinks are cold and hard facts. During various times in the deliberations he accuses his fellow jury members of being "bleeding hearts," or "old ladies," or both, and as being subject to emotional appeals. Ironically it is he who thinks mostly with his emotions. As the initial evidence is slowly overturned, he doggedly holds to the very end that the defendant is guilty, and is the last to change his mind. To his credit though, as the film concludes, he seems to undergo a genuine conversion and seems to make a confession of guilt, towards both the defendant and his own son, as he mutters softly while crying "not guilty, not guilty." Among all the jurors, he alone seems to have been transformed significantly by the deliberations. Lee J. Cobb's portrayal of Juror #3 is excellent. His acting electrifies the film and has a powerful influence on the viewer.

Juror #4 (Stockbroker played by E.G. Marshall): He is apparently a man of wealth and position. He is a somewhat prudish person who seems convinced of his own infallibility and also that he is above the common emotions of the ordinary man. The sweltering heat of the jury room seems to bother everyone else but him. He notes the weakness of the defendant's alibi, emphasizes the uniqueness of the knife used in the murder, and catches Juror #8 in an appeal to pity. Nevertheless, he is not above committing fallacies himself, for example, a red herring, when he objects to Juror #8's purchase of a similar knife to the one used in the murder, by remarking that it is illegal to possess such weapons.

Throughout the deliberations he remains calm and unemotional and tenaciously holds that the defendant is guilty based primarily upon one piece of evidence he regards as conclusive: the eyewitness testimony of the woman across the street from where the murder took place. Reasonably, he quickly changes his position when the retired man undermines her testimony with his observation that the woman had eyeglass marks on her nose. Since no one wears eyeglasses to bed, the jury concludes, with her vision thus impaired, she could have been mistaken about what she claims to have seen.

Juror #5 (Mechanic played by Jack Klugman): He is a somewhat defensive young man who asks if he can pass on the first go around of the deliberations. He shares a similar ethnic and economic background with the defendant and thus challenges the hasty generalization of Juror #10 about the "trash" who crawl out of the ghettos. Although he seems to find it difficult to disagree, he shows independent and critical thinking when he demonstrates the proper use of a switchblade knife, arguing that if the defendant had been the killer it would have been more likely that he would have stabbed upward, as is common with the use of such knives, rather than downward as occurred in the murder. He becomes more assertive as the deliberation progresses and defends the architect's argument that the lame, old man could not have walked to his apartment door quickly enough, in fifteen seconds, as he claimed, to see the defendant escaping down the stairs.

Juror #6 (House Painter played by Edward Binns): He is hardworking, but somewhat unsure of himself. He focuses on the fact that the boy had a motive for the murder. He seems ready to turn to violence, or at least threatens it, and thus commits the appeal to force fallacy in his defense of the retired man's right to speak. For the most part, he finds it difficult to form his own opinions. He says he is content to let his boss think for him. He commits the appeal to ignorance fallacy when he says to Juror #8, "I'm not one for supposing but suppose you convince us that the defendant is innocent but it turns out that he is really guilty and he goes on to kill again?" Thus, he uses the lack of evidence as evidence to make Juror #8 feel guilty about turning a merely suspected criminal into a real criminal who most likely will repeat his crime.

Juror #7 (Salesman played by Jack Warden): His main contribution to the deliberations is his noting of the defendant's prior history and criminal record. Otherwise this loud, flashy individual's only interest is to speed up the proceedings, justice or no justice, so he can be off in time to take in a baseball game. He resents the immigrant juror for suggesting that he, the salesman, does not understand the meaning of reasonable doubt. Resisting the immigrant's call to responsible decision making when he changes his vote for no good reason, he commits a hasty generalization by charging the immigrant and all other immigrants with attempting to run the whole show once they get to this country though only recently they had been running for their lives. The salesman thus plays the caricature role of the "ugly American," the typical dumb American chauvinist.

Juror #8 (Architect played by Henry Fonda): He is a man of obvious intellectual strength which is tempered with compassion. He is not perfect, nevertheless, and is caught by Juror #4, as noted earlier, committing the appeal to pity fallacy. After his solitary dissent at the initial preliminary ballot, he guides the remaining jurors through a somewhat explosive process that reveals the wobbly foundation of their convictions about the defendant's guilt. Under his criticisms and the observations of the retired man, each of the more important "facts" used as evidence against the defendant are undermined. The undermining of the initial evidence begins when Juror #8 demonstrates that the alleged unique knife, the murder weapon, is not really so when he, dramatically, sticks an identical knife into the jury room table. He then overturns the old man's testimony to have heard the boy yelling "I'm going to kill ya" before the father was stabbed by suggesting that for a full ten seconds before the body fell to the floor, the "el" train was simultaneously roaring by the apartment's window. Because the noise of the passing train would be so loud, it would have been impossible for anyone to have heard any yelling at all.

Juror #8 casts doubt on the fourth piece of evidence against the accused, that the defendant's alibi was weak since he could not remember the names of the films or actors of the movies he claims he saw when questioned by the police after he returns home. Given the highly emotional state the defendant would have been in upon just learning that his father had been murdered and that he laid dead in the adjoining room, the architect argues, such memory loss is to be expected. By way of analogy, he attempts to show that in these circumstances it would be natural to forget these details and demonstrates this when he questions the stockbroker about films he recently saw. He catches the stockbroker in a memory loss about the precise titles and names of the actors, while pointing out to his fellow jury members that the stockbroker's memory loss occurred while he was under no similar emotional stress as was the defendant at the time he was interrogated.

Juror #8 questions the old man's credibility in his claim that he saw the boy as he fled down the stairs when he paces out the distance from the old man's bed to his apartment's door and then with a reenactment demonstrates that, given the old man's lame condition, he could not have covered the distance in the fifteen seconds he claimed it took him to get to the door of his apartment. The architect convinces most of his fellow jurors that it would have taken the old man more than twice as long, and thus what he "saw" when he finally got there may have been someone he only thought was the boy.

One of the important contributions of the architect to the deliberations is his insistence to his fellow jurors that in the American legal system an individual accused of a crime should be presumed innocent until proven guilty. Frequently jurors, as do some in the film, demand incorrectly that the defendant prove himself or herself innocent, and in doing so, misplace the burden of proof, putting it on the defendant and not on the state where it belongs. As each of the initial pieces of evidence are weakened or overturned, the case for guilt is correspondingly undermined and the basis for a reasonable doubt is made more persuasive. Increasingly, the presumption of innocence and the weakened evidence requires that the boy be found not guilty.

Juror #9 (Retired Man played by Joseph Sweeney): He is an old man, frail and thin but with 20-20 vision and an uncanny power of observation for details, both psychological and physical. He notes tell-tale details that his fellow jurors miss and these turn out to be critical for their deliberations.

He notices, for example, that the old man who claims to have seen and heard the accused wore a torn jacket to court and seemed more interested in establishing his own importance rather than getting at the truth. With regard to the second eyewitness, the woman living across the street from where the murder took place, he notices that she was a forty-year-old woman trying hard to look thirty. And even more critically, he remembers that she had small marks on the sides of her nose, most likely made by the wearing of eye-glasses, even though she did not wear them to court, because, he speculates, she thought they would ruin her appearance. Furthermore, since she was in bed at the time of the murder, and most likely not wearing her glasses, her claim, with her vision thus impaired, that she saw the boy kill his father is called into doubt. She would have had to seen this occur from a distance of sixty feet away through the windows of a passing elevated ("el") train.

Many years of living and learning have brought the retired man, Juror #9, much wisdom and empathy for his fellow men. Without his keen observations, the jury most likely would have been declared hung, especially by those jurors who remained convinced by the eye-witness testimony of the woman from across the street where the murder occurred.

Juror #10 (Garage Owner played by Ed Begley): He is an angry, bitter man who seems to value everything only from an economical perspective, for example, he points out how much the trial is costing the taxpayer. He is filled with prejudice and spits like a battery syringe whenever the subject of race comes up. To his fellow jurors' credit, his racist views are rejected and he is symbolically ostracized at one point in the film when he goes on a lengthy tirade of bigotry. Besides the hasty generalizations which he makes, for example, that the members of the defendant's ethnic group are all liars and prone to violence, he is guilty of an appeal to popular sentiment fallacy, when he complains, "Boy, oh boy, there is always one" during the preliminary ballot, when Juror #8 casts the one dissenting vote. Ironically, towards the film's end, he is the one set apart and alone by his blatant racism. He is probably the most negative character among the jurors. If he is affected at all by the proceedings, it seems only by being amazed that his fellow jurors share neither his bigotry nor his concern about the "danger" he somehow apprehends in the members of the defendant's ethnic group.

Juror #11 (Watchmaker played by George Voskovec): He is a refugee from Europe. An intelligent man, he sees clearly that it is not only the boy who is on trial but the jury system itself and each of the jurors as well. He apparently lived in a totalitarian state and seems to have experienced first hand the loss of freedom and the corresponding oppression. He gives the impression of one who deeply appreciates the democratic principle on which the American jury system is based. He speaks with a slight accent and shares with the defendant the pain from the prejudice frequently expressed towards foreigners. He makes a case for the accused not being guilty with the following argument: that if the boy were the murderer, he would not have had the composure to wipe his fingerprints off the knife nor be so unwise as to return to the scene of the crime, given the fact that he heard the woman screaming from across the street and thus would have been aware that she saw him commit the crime. His argument, while somewhat convincing, is not found so by his fellow jurors.

Juror #12 (Advertising Man played by Robert Webber): He is a slick, bright but superficial man who cares more for packaging than substance. He has the dubious distinction of having changed his vote more than any other juror, three times—from guilty, to not guilty, back to guilty, and then back to not guilty. While making no specific contributions to the deliberations, nevertheless, he starts them off on a good footing when he suggests that the burden of proof lies with those who believe the defendant guilty. It is they, he rightly argues, who should present their reasons for their view to show the sole dissenter where he has gone wrong. But even when making this remark, a good one at that, he is afraid he has made a blunder and apologizes for it. As the film unfolds it becomes clear that he is out to please the crowd and be thought of as a good fellow. He seems to want to choose the safer, popular course rather than to become personally involved in the difficult and trying search for the truth without regard for who is displeased by it.

THE FILM'S RELEVANCE TODAY

12 Angry Men focuses on important social issues, ones which, unfortunately, even though it was released in 1957, remain relevant today. These issues are dramatically portrayed and made personal through complex characterization, and through the brilliant matching of the technical aspects of the film to subject matter. When Rose began writing *12 Angry Men*, he knew that his play could not exceed the fifty minutes allotted to the television show for which it was intended. Faced with this time constraint, he brilliantly and convincingly character types the twelve jurors, engrosses the viewer in the deliberations, and makes dramatic and significant statements about prejudice, the power of reason, and human nature generally, showing both its strengths and foibles.

As such the film can serve as an excellent tool for teaching critical thinking as it vividly demonstrates the pitfalls of prejudices and hasty generalizations. In addition to its making social issues real rather than abstract and remote, the film shows the darker side of the human psyche, as well as the complexity and subtlety of human motivation, often, not remediable, unfortunately, by a mere appeal to reason.

While the film does end on a positive note, several questions remain: What would have happened if Juror #8 had not expressed his dissent? How many juries have allowed deep-seated prejudices to interfere with their judgment? What chance of an unbiased decision has a defendant who is racially, socially, ethnically, religiously or politically deviant? In part, because it raises these troubling questions, about the ultimate fairness and reliability of the jury system itself, the film has retained its emotional and educational impact over the years.

The emotional outbursts which punctuate the story serve as reminders that jury decisions are not always made by objective thinking. This is what makes the film so unsettling. It becomes clear how close this jury came to committing a grave error, and we see that it is quite possible that others like it might err in the future. We wonder and worry about how many current and future juries can be so blasé about the risk of putting an innocent person to death. And while the jurors in *12 Angry Men* fortunately have avoided this terrible error, one wonders if they really have learned from the experience. Some may have, especially Juror #3, as we noted earlier, but one suspects that for most, their experience simply might become a memory they choose to forget.

If the film does nothing else, it reminds us, like a catechism, of the function and responsibility of jury persons to think carefully and critically when considering the evidence presented to them. By way of criticism, perhaps the film rests too much faith on the presence of an open-minded individual, who will, as did the architect, single-handedly look at all the evidence, spot inconsistency and turn his fellow jurors away from a grave error and towards the truth. In *12 Angry Men* reason wins out over unreason. But it makes one wonder how easy, under similar circumstances, a miscarriage of justice can occur in our system. Perhaps this is the single most important moral the author, Reginald Rose, intended his story to teach. Over-all, the film remains, despite its somewhat excessive confidence in the independent power of rational thinking, a very effective and useful way to teach critical thinking.

Twelve Angry Men Presents an Idealized View of the Jury System

David Burnell Smith

The 1957 film version of *Twelve Angry Men* is a good, entertaining piece of cinematography, but it has multiple inaccurate portrayals of real justice. From this thesis titled "Reel Justice: The Movies' View of the American Legal System," David Burnell Smith uses multiple sources to both praise the film and reveal its inaccuracies.

Reginald Rose wrote his award-winning play "Twelve Angry Men" in [1954]. [It was unlikely that] this compelling, sober study of a jury deliberating a murder case could ever be made into a motion picture. All the action of the play took place in a jury room and there were no exterior settings. No romantic scenes were portrayed. This was a character drama with powerful dialogue. The play was successful and the screen version was even more successful, confounding the skeptics.

Celebrated director Sidney Lumet wanted to make "Twelve Angry Men" into a movie.* Lumet was fascinated by the detailed study of twelve men playing God and deciding the fate of a defendant accused of murder. He also wanted to show the American public how the jury system worked. Lumet brought together some of New York's finest character actors for his movie version—Lee J. Cobb, Ed Begley, Jack Klugman, Jack Warden, E.G. Marshall, and one of Hollywood's most respected performers, Henry Fonda. Lumet utilized closeups and unusual camera angles to help sustain

---

*Actually, it was actor Henry Fonda who initially approached Reginald Rose about making "Twelve Angry Men" into a film after its 1954 television broadcast. Fonda and Rose decided to coproduce the film. They then hired Sidney Lumet, an experienced stage and television director, who had no film experience, to direct the movie.

Excerpted from "Reel Justice: The Movies' View of the American Legal System," a thesis by David Burnell Smith (Reno: University of Nevada, 1995). Reprinted with permission of the author.

the tension and the conflict of the plot. Lumet made the decision to shoot the entire film in an actual jury room. His direction won acclaim and the film would be studied for years to come.

THE PLOT

The plot is simple. The jury is deliberating the fate of a young, poor Puerto Rican who is accused of the switchblade murder of his father in their ghetto apartment in New York. The case appears to be open and shut. The evidence and the motive are clear. The defendant is obviously guilty. Or is he? Eleven of the jurors think he is. However, one of the jurors, played by Fonda, firmly believes the opposite. If this were a real trial, it would surely end up as a hung jury because it would be highly unlikely that the eleven could be convinced by the lone dissenter. However, the story here defies that logic. The task is for the lone dissenter to change the minds of all eleven. There are at least three jurors as strongly committed to a guilty verdict as Fonda is to a verdict of not guilty.

Fonda sees all the evidence as circumstantial. He sees holes in the prosecution's argument. He sees the defense attorneys as incredibly ineffective. He even states, "It is also possible for a lawyer to be just plain stupid, isn't it? I mean, it's possible." From that beginning, Fonda works to convince the eleven men, one by one. The first convert comes easily. He is an elderly man who sides with Fonda simply because he admires his willingness to fight for something for which he believes.

Throughout the drama, Fonda works the jury by using logic and then emotion to cast doubt on the guilt of this young man. Writer Reginald Rose never tells the audience whether the defendant is guilty or not. He suggests that it's enough that he should be presumed innocent and then uses Fonda's character to make that case. The "Angry" of the title is appropriate because Rose manages to elicit anger and frustration from all twelve men in his drama. A few of the jurors want to get the case decided since it is apparent that the kid is guilty. Fonda says, "We can't decide in five minutes. Suppose we're wrong?" He then attacks the incompetent defense attorney, saying, "If I was on trial for my life, I'd want my lawyer to tear the prosecution witness to shreds, or at least try to."

Fonda's chief adversary is Lee J. Cobb, a formidable,

tough, abrasive and obstinate foe. Cobb states his case. "We're trying to put a guilty man in the chair where he belongs." Fonda also receives antagonism from Ed Begley, who states, "You're not going to change anybody's mind." E.G. Marshall fights Fonda with cold and determined logic. For almost two hours of screen time, the magnificent Fonda wards off arguments from his adversaries as he continues to convert the others. Finally, he converts the stubborn and mean-spirited Cobb. Fonda's performance is restrained. He is convincing. He is a stalwart for justice.

Here Fonda is the leader and not the follower that he was in *The Ox-Bow Incident*. His performance is one of the biggest reasons why the premise of *Twelve Angry Men* works. He convinces the movie audience that he has persuaded the other members of the jury. He also subtly condemns capital punishment as he attacks the possibility of an innocent boy who might be wrongly convicted. In a highly charged scene, Fonda and Cobb clash. Cobb says, "What's the matter with you guys? You all know he's guilty. He's got to burn. You're letting him slip through our fingers." Fonda replies, "Slip through our fingers? Are you his executioner?" Cobb angrily reacts, "I'm one of them." Fonda goads him, "Perhaps you'd like to pull the switch?" Cobb readily concurs, "For this kid, you bet I would." This sets up Fonda's character for the final criticism, "What it must feel like to want to pull the switch. Ever since you walked into this room you have acted like a self-appointed public avenger. You want to see this boy die because you personally want it. Not because of the facts. You're a sadist."

If New York had not had the death penalty in 1957 perhaps Rose wouldn't have written his play. The excitement and tension of *Twelve Angry Men* works best as the audience sees a life at stake and the jury playing God. The jury acts as a prominent force.

Twelve Angry Men ends with the acquittal of the defendant thanks to the persistence of one courageous man. "Reel" justice here shows that the jury system works and one person can make a difference.

"REEL" JUSTICE

Twelve Angry Men is well made and well acted. It is produced with passion and commitment. However, some would say it is a distortion of legal reality. In *American Film Maga-*

zine, Alan Dershowitz says, "It is an important movie for potential jurors to see. It brings home to them the need for an open mind."[1] He then proceeds to criticize the film's inaccuracies. Of course, the biggest inaccuracy is the plot itself, the idea that one person in a murder case can change the minds of eleven jurors.

Seymour Wishman in his well documented book, *Anatomy of a Jury,* points out that no case like that, of a lone dissenter who turns the jury around in *Twelve Angry Men,* ever cropped up in the study of over two thousand jurors. *The Chicago Jury Project* is a study of 255 trials. It discovered that two out of ten juries unanimously voted on the first ballot for conviction, and one out of ten voted for acquittal. In other words, deliberations ended after the first ballot in three out of ten cases. This same study also found that 95% of the time the majority on the first ballot prevailed. Five percent of the remaining cases, in which a minority prevailed, revealed that there were always three or four jurors in the minority and never a lone dissenter as in *Twelve Angry Men.*

The jury studies show that deliberations are normally short in duration. Seymour Wishman points out, ". . . by the time jurors go into the jury room to deliberate, they have made up their minds."[2] A future juror might rent a video of *Twelve Angry Men* and come to the conclusion that he or she will do exactly what Fonda did and adamantly oppose the eleven others. Unfortunately, in real life, a lone dissenter would not likely be able to change the minds of eleven others. It would probably result in a hung jury. *The Chicago Jury Project* also points out that contrary to popular belief, "hung juries are not usually caused by a single stubborn juror, but by the closeness of the case and by the moral commitment jurors feel when their minority view has several supporters."[3]

As dramatic fiction, *Twelve Angry Men* is a fine work. But it remains fiction. It is another example of Hollywood's distortion of what truly happens in American courtrooms. Ultimately, Henry Fonda is an exaggerated form of a super hero, not the average man that he is intended to be.

Although Dershowitz believes potential jurors should see *Twelve Angry Men,* he denounces a scene in the film in which jurors talk about the weapon found in the body. It is supposedly a unique switchblade with one of a kind design. Fonda suddenly reaches in his pocket and pulls out a knife.

He opens it and thrusts it into the top of the juror's table. It is an exact duplicate. Dershowitz points out that jurors cannot bring their own evidence into the jury room and indeed they are specifically forbidden from doing so. This is a critical part of the plot because it is the major reason the arguments of the eleven begin to fall. The bringing of the knife into the jury room would be illegal and result in a mistrial.

IDEALISM, NOT REALITY

Thomas J. Harris, in his book *Courtroom's Finest Hour*, says that Rose's screen play is, on the whole, an angered denunciation of the American public's idealistic approach to the reality of the system. Harris asserts that the American public has an idealistic view of many aspects of democracy, and *Twelve Angry Men* portrays the jury system as working. Harris clarifies this statement when he refers to Rose, saying, "His message, that the law is no better than the people who enforce it, and that the people who enforce it are all too human. . . ."[4]

Twelve Angry Men, in the broader sense, is not only about a murder trial and the determination of one man to do the right thing, it is a detailed look at the judicial system itself. The judicial system is placed on trial on the screen. In this instance, the movie shows that the system works. It only works, however, because one special man fights the majority rule.

"Reel" justice in this movie shows that one person can stand against the majority and win. *Twelve Angry Men* espouses the thought that the jury system works and that right will triumph over wrong if commitment and determination are used to seek out the truth.

FOOTNOTES

1. Alan Dershowitz, "Legal Eagles," *American Film Magazine*, November 1986, p. 59.
2. Seymour Wishman, *Anatomy of a Jury*. New York: Times Books, 1986, p. 237.
3. Wishman, *Anatomy of a Jury*, p. 237.
4. Thomas J. Harris, *Courtroom's Finest Hour in American Cinema*. Metuchen, NJ: Scarecrow Press, 1987, p. 21.

An Unconvincing Film with an Important Message

Thomas J. Harris

Author Thomas J. Harris commends screenwriter Reginald Rose for the "convincing account of how a liberal man who is devoted to his cause is able to sway the ignorant and prejudiced minds of his peers." But he criticizes Rose for an overreliance on Juror #8 as the lone source of good, for that results in details being too easily exposed and too simply clarified. Yet despite this and other shortcomings in the film, "there is no denying that it is brilliantly tight, that it makes for exhilarating drama, and that it is food for thought."

[At the end of the story,] we see that in the beginning this group of diverse individuals was prepared (with the exception of [Juror 8, Henry] Fonda) to send a boy to the chair and then go home and forget all about it. It is frightening to consider just how close they came to doing so. It must be stated, however, that the jury's final verdict of not-guilty does not prove conclusively that the boy did not murder his father; rather, the script shows that the case against the boy is not as strong as the case for him—the presence of reasonable doubt is [screenwriter Reginald] Rose's concern.

CONCERNS ABOUT REALISM

What if there had been no Juror 8? Rose may be praised for his convincing account of how a liberal man who is devoted to his cause is able to sway the ignorant and prejudiced minds of his peers. However, at the same time it may be said that the script relies too heavily upon the chance presence of such a man; if he had not been there to point out evidence that no one else had been able to produce, the boy would presumably have been sent to the chair. It is also questionable whether such a man, even if he happened to be present, would have the stamina to enable him to ignore the incessant badgering of his colleagues—as one character in the film remarks, "It isn't easy to stand up to the ridicule of others." Indeed, because the story "is based on the dramatically convenient but otherwise simplistic assumption that people's prejudices can be traced to specific occurrences in their past and can thereby be accounted for and removed . . . the Fonda character had to come on as a combination Sherlock Holmes and Perry Mason, as well as double as confessor, catalyst, and instant psychiatrist to a number of the jurors."[1] Also, due to the great reliance upon Fonda's presence, details are exposed and clarified much too smoothly. It is only Fonda who employs logical reasoning most of the time, and even when someone else brings up a point it usually comes as the result of Fonda's questioning. It may also be stated that, as Adam Garbicz and Jacek Klinowski remark in their article on the film in *Cinema: The Magic Vehicle*, "the actors are hardly a team, but rather a group of diverse individuals against whom Henry Fonda shines with all the more brightness."[2] . . .

In addition to the issue of the omniscience of the Fonda character, the script eschews realism for dramatic convenience in other respects also. Juror 3's sudden emotional breakdown, for example, remains largely unconvincing because it is triggered by the chance appearance of a photo of him and his son when he throws the wallet down on the table. Since all the others have sided with Fonda, Rose is left with no alternative but to find a quick and easy method for getting Juror 3 to do the same.

LEGITIMATE CRITICISMS OF THE JURY SYSTEM

Nevertheless, Rose does manage to point out ironic truths about the judicial system on a reasonably frequent basis. There is, for example, the bigot's complaint that the old man is "twisting the facts" when he says that the elderly gentleman on the stand gave testimony mainly to look distinguished. Since the jurors are not the people on the stand, they cannot know what the witnesses are thinking; hence, the truth is often never revealed. The best the jury can do is try to read between the lines and make intelligent guesses; however, we have seen that initially no one except Fonda even considered the possibility of testimony being inaccurate.

JUROR #8 IS CLEARLY NEITHER IMPARTIAL NOR WITHOUT FAULT

Northern Illinois University professor of speech communi-cation Russell Proctor uses the 1957 film Twelve Angry Men *as a classroom teaching aid. However, multiple viewing has caused him to conclude that the story's hero is not quite pure in all of his tactics.*

On the surface, the moral of the story seems to be that good triumphs over evil through the efforts of a heroic critical thinker. . . . Henry Fonda raises questions, encourages quiet members to offer their opinions, and fights against the tyranny of bigotry. . . .

After repeated viewings of the movie, however, I became in-creasingly troubled by some of Fonda's tactics. Though he en-gages in critical thinking about *some* issues, his logic is ex-tremely poor about others. He rewards only the jurors who agree with him and berates those who disagree; clearly he is *not* impartial. Group pressure, which works against him at the outset of the story, is the primary tool Fonda uses to get his adversaries to capitulate. By attending to the maintenance needs of quiet jurors who would be overmatched without his support, Fonda turns the tide of conformity in his favor. The moral of the story is not necessarily the triumph of good over evil, for the defendant's innocence is unclear at the film's con-clusion. Instead, what the story demonstrates is that persua-sion in groups can take place through a variety of methods—and Fonda's method is as worthy of critical scrutiny as any of the others employed during the jury's deliberations.

Russell F. Proctor II, "Do the Ends Justify the Means? Thinking Critically About *Twelve Angry Men*," April 14, 1991.

There is also the fact that the presence of certain individ-uals in the jury room can alter the course of events. No one except Juror 5, who was once a slum kid, knows how a switchblade is handled. He demonstrates how awkward it would have been for the boy, who was much shorter than his father, to stab upward into the chest. The old man, pre-occupied with studying people his own age, deduces from his observations of the vain woman in the witness box that she wasn't wearing her glasses.

Rose leaves it up to the viewer whether the experience of being a jury member has changed the characters of the men who have been shown their true selves as a result. It appears as though the bigot and the bully have confronted deep-seated personal conflicts for the first time in their lives. One wonders, however, whether the lessons they learned in court will have a long-term effect on their perceptions of the world. . . .

CINEMATIC CONTRIBUTIONS

In terms of cinematic execution, *12 Angry Men* was clearly a film of its time. It is probable that if it were made today under the same conditions (with a TV crew and at TV speed), audiences who have since come to accept motion pictures and television as two unique forms of entertainment—with much higher standards for films—would dismiss it as a laughable "gimmick" film despite the gravity of its messages.

Nevertheless, after nearly thirty years *12 Angry Men* remains one of the most absorbing exposés of the workings of the judicial process. This is due mainly to Rose's penetrating indictment of the reliability of the jury system. [Director Sidney] Lumet's contribution was pretty much technical (although his direction of the actors was superlative); indeed, what with the challenge of having to complete the shooting in a mere twenty days, he could hardly have been expected to develop any sort of personal philosophy. Although the film ends on a happy note, the viewer (as mentioned before) is inescapably reminded of the more serious implications of the previous ninety minutes: the extent to which personal biases can taint a juror's perceptions of the real issues and as a result endanger the lives of the (presumably innocent) parties on trial. Even though Rose does not offer alternatives to the present system of trial by jury, his screenplay is, on the whole, a more fervent and angered denunciation of the American public's idealistic approach to the reliability of the system. His message, that "the law is no better than the people who enforce it, and that the people who enforce it are all too human,"[3] is just as pertinent today as it was in 1957.

FOOTNOTES

1. Jean-Pierre Coursodon and Pierre Sauvage, "Sidney Lumet," in *American Directors*, vol. 2 (New York: McGraw-Hill, 1983), p. 209.
2. Adam Garbicz and Jack Klinowski, *Cinema, the Magic Vehicle: A Guide to Its Achievement*, vol. 2 (New York: Schocken Books, 1983), p. 299.
3. *Time*, April 29, 1957, p. 96.

CHAPTER 3

Critical Reviews of *Twelve Angry Men*

READINGS ON

TWELVE ANGRY MEN

The 1954 Production Was Excellent Television Drama

Leonard Traube

Studio One, a weekly anthology series on television, premiered "Twelve Angry Men" on September 20, 1954. This review of the original "Twelve Angry Men" ran in *Variety* magazine on September 22, 1954; the critic, Leonard Traube, regularly reviewed television programs for *Variety*. The original broadcast was obviously noteworthy, for Traube wrote, "Seldom in TV history has a story been able to achieve so many high points with such frequency and maintain the absorbing, tense pace. . . . The play was a whammo."

"Studio One" is fortunate with its numbers. . . . On [September 20] it led off [its 1954] season with "Twelve Angry Men," by the same Reginald Rose who gave you such other . . . works as "Remarkable Incident at Carson Corners," "Thunder On Sycamore Street" and "The Death and Life of Larry Benson."

"Twelve Angry Men" was a wallop on all main counts—script and performances; direction (by Franklin Schaffner, who's rotating on the series with Paul Nickell) and in Felix Jackson's correct conception of the production as an eloquent suspense vehicle. For the viewer at large who's not much concerned—nor should he be—with the technical niceties, the impact was in the playing, meshed strikingly with a masterly example of television lensing, and in the superior staging. Here was a troupe of six names and as many featured thesps (no baker's dozen but sum total of cast) brought together not merely for the marquee values but as picked emoters alive to their special characterizations as members of a jury deliberating in a murder case.

Excerpted from "Studio One," by Leonard Traube, *Variety,* September 22, 1954. Reprinted by permission of *Variety* magazine.

Seldom in TV history has a story been able to achieve so many high points with such frequency and maintain the absorbing, tense pace. Limited to the jury room (except for the opening with a brief flash of the bench charging the panel), the playout scored impact after impact as the plain and not so plain joes struggled with their consciences and with each other to arrive at a just verdict.

Atmosphere of tension and the vagaries of the human mind were established almost immediately with a vote of 11-1 for guilty—Robert Cummings casting the "not." From here in playwright Rose developed the reasons why "12 good men and true" are caused to alter their opinions, building point-by-point on the available and post-charge evidence and testimony. Each man had his series of says, Franchot Tone and Edward Arnold as the last of the holdouts in dynamic performances; Paul Hartman, with a deft light characterization of a joeblow typical of many a juryman; John Beal, the quiet one; Walter Abel, the natty articulate logician; Cummings, the fair-minded sole dissenter in the beginning whose points and tactics are the final persuader in acquittal; and interesting studies of men groping to do the right thing in the exceptionally skilled performances of George Voskovec, Lee Philips, Joseph Sweeney, Will West, Bart Burns and Norman Feld.

If a number of faults could be found, one was in the remarkable fact that, considering some of the conscionable struggles of the panel, the defense attorney must have been asleep in not citing the salient points brought out within the private confines of the jury room. But this is carping. The play was whammo.

Twelve Angry Men Is a Shallow Call to Civic-Mindedness

Jonathan Baumbach

In this 1957 film review, Jonathan Baumbach calls
Twelve Angry Men a good film but laments that it
could have been a better one. He accuses screenwriter Reginald Rose of too cleanly wrapping up the
story at the end and sweeping the weightier implications into the cracks. Baumbach criticizes the film
because no changes are advocated for the obvious
systematic flaws that it brings to light. Jonathan
Baumbach is a professor of English at Brooklyn
College of the City University of New York (CUNY),
where he coordinates the fiction division. He is the
author of twelve books of fiction, one of nonfiction,
and eighty published short stories. He has twice
been the Chairman of the National Center of film
Critics. He wrote this review while a student at
Columbia University.

Television, among its multitudinous sins and nominal
virtues, succeeded [in the 1950s] in developing a new genre
in drama made respectable by a half dozen reasonably serious playwrights. It is an especial genre created out of the
needs and specifications of an especial medium. Though
each of the television writers is a separate, thinking entity
unto the others, and though there is reputedly little or no
collaboration between them, one finds in all of their work,
no matter how different the ostensible premise, the common
denominator of the medium. This is particularly in evidence
when a television play is transplanted to the stage or film.

Reginald Rose, who adapted his own television play
Twelve Angry Men for the screen, is the "social conscious"
representative of the clan. In *Twelve Angry Men*, Rose, with

Excerpted from *"Twelve Angry Men,"* by Jonathan Baumbach, *Film Culture*, 1957.
Reprinted with permission from the author.

journalistic concern for precise detail, explores the processes of justice and injustice in an American jury trial. Since the entire action of the film takes place in the jury room where twelve laymen debate the life of an 18-year-old boy accused of killing his father, the film is among other things a tour de force of craftsmanship for Mr. Rose and director Sidney Lumet. It is a tribute to their combined ingenuity that the piece is always compelling and at moments even moving. The cast, including Lee J. Cobb, Henry Fonda, E.G. Marshall, and Jack Warden, is an exceptional one and gives the film added weight and breadth.

BENEATH THE SHINY SURFACE

Twelve Angry Men is undoubtedly a melodrama of the first rank if one is willing to accept it solely on its presentational level, but the ramifications of its theme lead one to search beneath its shiny surface—and on this less solid ground the film must be discussed.

At the outset, we have twelve hot and tired jurors crowded in a small, airless room in a New York City Court House to decide the fate of a teen-aged child of the slums obviously of some minority group (although particular references are scrupulously avoided). The boy has been accused with eye-witness verification of knifing his father, and eleven of his twelve appointed peers are convinced of his guilt. Only Juror Number 8, played with quiet dignity by Henry Fonda, has a reasonable doubt of the youngster's guilt. He wants to "talk a little." The others are furious. Juror Number 10 (the bigot), played by Ed Begley, expresses it: "There's always one in a crowd." A non-conformist, a rebel, a disinterested seeker after justice—one of the angels! As the action unravels in a frenetic series of fire cracker pops, we are led into gradual recognition of each member of the jury as a stereotypical member of our society. Juror Number 1 (the foreman) is an easy-going, non-thinking member of the majority; Number 2 is a meek bank clerk who is undoubtedly a tiger in his dream world; Number 3 is a pathological child-hater, avenging himself vicariously on a runaway "ungrateful" son; Number 4 is a non-sweating, smug and superior stock broker with a religious belief in his own omniscience; Number 5 is a shy, sensitive man who, despite his slum origin, has become a productive citizen; Number 6 is a well-meaning truck driver (a symbol, perhaps, of the dignity of labor);

"Injustices and Outrages Bothered Me"

Excerpts from this 1982 interview with playwright Reginald Rose present both his motivation and a self-critique of his work in the Twelve Angry Men *era.*

"The things I used to write about [in the 1950s and '60s] all involved violence," said Rose. . . . Blacks were being thrown out of their homes, there were all kinds of different attitudes over what social issues were. So many of the things I wrote about in those days were burning issues. Injustices and outrages that I saw bothered me. I saw them and I wanted to fight against them. I wanted to get them out of my system.

"Now what I do [in 1982] is different. I don't know whether it's softer but I think it is far more subtle. I know that it goes into depths far more than those early things. They were good, I think, but they were—I shouldn't use the word 'caricatures,' but perhaps they were superficial somewhat or surface things, as well as dealing with social issues.

"But they were more adventurous than an examination of relationships. That's a strange thing to say about my work, because that's not what I do generally."

Rex Polier, "Reflections on TV's Golden Age," *Los Angeles Times*, January 1, 1982.

Number 7 is a successful free-lance salesman, representing one of the lower orders of humanity; Number 8 is an architect, a man of reason who is not afraid to stand alone; Number 9 is a seemingly ordinary old man but one with great wisdom in his heart; Number 10 is also one of the lower orders—an unpleasantly bigoted Babbit; Number 11 is a naturalized American with a deep awareness of his newly acquired responsibilities and rights; and Number 12 is a Madison Avenue advertising man—a light-headed lightweight. As soon as positions are established we have a line-up of devils on one side and angels on the other. There is no incisive characterization . . . but only a tidy melodramatic battle of wits between the thinking and the fairminded and the unthinking and narrow minded.

EXPLORATION WITHOUT DISCOVERY

Doing his courageous best, Mr. Rose comes out unequivocally on the side of the angels. The film is resolved cleanly like a 300-piece cardboard jigsaw puzzle. The weightier implications, however, are not so easily swept into the cracks—Rose explores but never truly discovers; he accepts homilies in lieu of rather more complex truths. The film is filled with all of those small homey bits of quasi-naturalism that television audiences have come to recognize as "just like real life." Moreover, Rose's comment is too general, too obviously on the side of right (as if one always knew what right is) to make a meaningful contribution. What he says, in essence, is that jury duty is a highly serious business and must be taken with a sense of trust and responsibility. Rose's social drama is, in actuality, civic-mindedness in fancy dress. No changes are advocated; these are social problems within an accepted framework of government. *Twelve Angry Men* is on the side of the angels, but only the very tame and respectable ones. It is a film which skirts the edges of such interesting ideas as the illusory nature of truth, the uneasy business of taking a man's life in legal retribution for crime, the problem of how to fix morality in a slum environment—but it avoids, in fear or wisdom, facing them head on. It is a good film. If only it were a better one.

Sidney Lumet . . . uses the camera with an instinctive eye for detail. The picture is full of significant moments pinpointed through close-ups, and evidence is presented visually like clues in a murder mystery. Much of this is inventive and exciting, but, when used to excess, the symbols planted like early Spring flowers emerge, unfortunately, as wax imitations. One scene in particular (and I stress it because the majority of Lumet's tricks are successful) miscarries badly. When Juror Number 10 (the bigot) regurgitates his prejudice with a kind of sick compulsion, each of the jurors, in order of sensibility, leaves the table and ritualistically turns his back. It is a piece of symbolic choreography harshly discordant in the realistic frame of the film.

Within its simplicity there is a freshness and ingenuousness about *Twelve Angry Men* uncommon in a slickly sophisticated film industry. It's as if Rose truly believed that there is a saint in every crowd—and that justice will, finally, out. In any event, one leaves the film with a good feeling.

Twelve Angry Men Questions the Possibility of Receiving a Fair Trial

James J. Desmarais

Twelve Angry Men focuses on "one of democracy's most sacred myths": the jury system. While not exactly an attack, the film questions the ultimate fairness and reliability of such a system. Although the story ends on a positive note, author James J. Desmarais points out that the process leaves unsettling questions. What if there had been no Juror #8? How many juries have allowed their prejudices to affect their decisions? In avoiding these issues, the film seems to imply that the system works as long as people of conviction are involved in it.

The 1950's are often referred to as the "Golden Age" of television because of the abundance of live television drama during that period. Unfortunately, many of the programs of that decade are lost. However, one of the best, "Twelve Angry Men," which was initially broadcast as a *Studio One* presentation in 1954, was later remade as a film in 1957. The film version of this Reginald Rose teleplay was largely a result of the influence of Henry Fonda, who was its star as well as its coproducer (with Reginald Rose). Director Sidney Lumet, a man experienced in television, had never directed a feature film before. The remainder of the cast was made up of some of the best actors in television, including E.G. Marshall, Ed Begley, Lee J. Cobb, Jack Warden, and Martin Balsam.

The film centers on one of democracy's most sacred myths: the jury system. While not exactly an attack, the film questions the ultimate fairness and reliability of such a system. With the exception of a short introductory scene inside

Excerpted from "*Twelve Angry Men*," by James J. Desmarais, in *Magill's Survey of Cinema, English Language Films*, first series, vol. 4, 1980, edited by Frank N. Magill (Englewood Cliffs, NJ: Salem Press, 1980). Copyright ©1980 by Frank N. Magill. Reprinted by permission of The Gale Group.

the courtroom and one closing scene outside the court building, the film centers entirely on what happens within the closed jury room. It is the process that these twelve jurors go through in determining the defendant's guilt or innocence which makes the film so engrossing.

A Fair Trial?

The Constitution of the United States guarantees everyone a fair and speedy trial before one's peers. Screenwriter Reginald Rose, however, questions both the practicality and feasibility of such a jury through his script. The defendant is an uneducated, teenaged Puerto Rican slum dweller. The "peers" who compose his jury are white, generally middle-aged, middle-class males. Nevertheless, these men have been chosen to decide whether he lives or dies. The script further suggests that these men, in addition to being socially, culturally, economically, and racially divergent, are, more importantly, indifferent.

Fortunately, there is one man (Henry Fonda) who instinctively feels the young man may be innocent. When the first vote is taken, he alone votes for acquittal. He does not do so because he is sure he is right but because he alone fears he may be wrong. The others, eager to help him reach the "right" decision, decide to review the case against the boy. Finally, Fonda agrees not to stand in the way if no other juror feels there is a possibility that the boy is innocent. However, if anyone wavers, then the others must agree to see it through to the end. Another vote is taken, and this time another juror votes for acquittal. Angered and frustrated, the jury begins the process of debating the case.

Initially, the case against the youth looks strong, but step by step Fonda introduces a question of doubt. Since the law states that this is all that is necessary to acquit a defendant, convincing the other members of the jury that there is such a question becomes the focus of the remainder of the film. Fonda must overcome the prejudice and personal hatred held by each of the members of the jury. Nevertheless, each piece of evidence is examined and questioned until slowly each member begins to accept the possibility of innocence. Finally, when evidence no longer supports a guilty verdict, a few members must face the reality that their personal prejudices have overtaken their reason. Eventually, the initial vote of guilty is reversed, leaving only one man in favor of that verdict. However, after a heartrending display of personal frustration, he, too, reverses his vote to make it unanimous for acquittal.

While the film ends on a positive note, the process leaves questions. What if there had been no Henry Fonda? How many juries have allowed deep-seated prejudices to inter-

---

TWELVE ANGRY MEN REVEALS THE THREATS TO TRUE DEMOCRACY

As a reaction to the anti-Communist investigations of Senator Joseph McCarthy in the early 1950s, which gave rise to the hearings of the U.S. House of Representatives Un-American Activities Committee, Twelve Angry Men *probes the idea that our nation is built on active citizenship.*

Twelve Angry Men can be characterized as a classic liberal response to the McCarthyist assault on American pluralism and tolerance which had scarred the country in the previous decade. . . .

Yet *Twelve Angry Men* is not so much a film about individual character—it is rather a probing of ideals in a country built upon the idea of active citizenship. The jurors function precisely as representatives of the American people in the pursuit of Justice (here added to Life, Liberty and the Pursuit of Happiness), a multibodied American Everyman: the sportsfanatic, the former slum-kid, the Swiss-German immigrant, the educated doctor, the advertising man, the self-made businessmen, the bigot. As symbolic representatives even names are unnecessary. . . .

The film peels the jury apart in search of a common bedrock, and the revelation of threats to true democracy. From an overconcern with leisure (the sports fan's tickets for the game), empty images (the advertising man with no point of view), to outright bigotry (juror 10's McCarthyist "these people are dangerous" outburst near the end functioning as a revelation of naked prejudice that is pointedly ignored by a jury finally refinding its democratic soul) the threats are revealed and overcome. And it is important that it is those arguably closest to the *spirit* of the American ideal—the "poor, tired and homeless"—who first take juror 8's cue to defend it. In particular, it is the immigrant juror 11 who makes the link between the jury and democracy, the practice and the Ideal, reminding America of its promise.

Norman Miller, "Twelve Angry Men," in Nicholas Thomas, *International Dictionary of Films and Filmmakers,* 2nd ed., 1990.

fere with their judgment? What chance of an unbiased decision has a defendant who is racially, socially, ethnically, religiously, or politically deviant? The film has retained its
emotional impact over the years because it raises these
questions.

Cinematically, the film effectively captures the claustrophobic atmosphere of the jury room. The characters complain incessantly about the humidity and stifling lack of air.
The tension and irritation generated by the proceedings further help to create an uncomfortable environment. The
room becomes a pressure cooker ready to burst from the
pent-up energies inside.

The film is a powerful and emotional experience. As is often the case when a teleplay is transferred to film, the
strengths remain with the writers and actors. Live television
was a writer's medium. Because the plays were broadcast
live, visuals were kept simple. Television was not afforded
the luxury of making mistakes. Therefore, the thrust was on
performance of the written word.

In the transition of *Twelve Angry Men* from television to
film little was changed, and as a result, the film is often
accused of appearing staged. However, considering the environment in which the story takes place, the film can be ex-
cused for not being visually diverse. The emotional outbursts which punctuate the story serve as reminders that
decisions are not always made by the brain but often by the
emotions. This is what makes the film ultimately so unsettling. It becomes clear how close these men came to committing a grave error, and we see that it is quite possible that
they and others like them might err in the future. The experience has been one of consequence for these men. Some
have been affected in such a way that it seems impossible for
them ever to be the same. Nonetheless, one wonders if they
really have learned from the experience. They have been
persuaded for today, but what about tomorrow? One suspects that their experience might simply become a memory
they choose to forget.

In many ways, the film is an indictment of the American
thought process in the 1950's. The jurors in *Twelve Angry
Men* are initially very confident in their decision to find the
man guilty. However, after being forced to think and recon-
sider the evidence against the youth, it becomes apparent
that they have not put as much thought into their decision as

one might hope. Their confidence in the American system of justice has blinded them to the possibility that it may have inherent weaknesses which affect the ability of some citizens to receive a fair trial. Nevertheless, because one man has the courage of his convictions, justice prevails. Idealistic optimism suggests that as long as there are good men, the system will succeed. This may ultimately be the film's message.

Twelve Angry Men Is a Cinematic Success

Leslie Halliwell

Translating a television screenplay to the big screen was a cinemographic feat, writes British film critic Leslie Halliwell. In the following review, Halliwell analyzes the elements that contributed to the film's success, and he notes how the subject matter is both uncomfortable and memorable. Halliwell has been a professional film critic since 1959. He writes the annual *Halliwell's Film and Video Guide*, and his *Halliwell's Filmgoer's Companion* published its twelfth edition in 1997.

One would not expect it to be cinematic at all. A celebrated piece of live television, which means that it was primarily a matter of talking heads, it was filmed almost exactly as originally devised, except that there was now more time to get the detail and the composition right. Apart from the briefest of scenes at beginning and end, there is only one set, and that is a bare and unlovely room big enough for a large oblong table and twelve chairs. At the far end, behind a glass partition, is a toilet and washroom. Outside the grimy windows we are made to feel the sweltering air of New York on a muggy day when thunderstorms constantly threaten and eventually make good that threat, darkening the room and making it even more oppressive.

Here twelve strangers meet, after sitting side by side in court for a week. Their mission is to discuss a case we have not seen tried and to come to a decision as to the defendant's guilt or innocence. Everything we learn about him and his supposed crime comes from their conversation, and to follow the nuances of character and the exactitude of evidence requires careful attention. The trouble is amply repaid, for this is a film which lodges itself uncomfortably in the mem-

Excerpted from *Halliwell's Hundred: A Nostalgic Choice of Films from the Golden Age*, by Leslie Halliwell. Copyright ©1982 by Leslie Halliwell. Reprinted by permission of Scribner, a division of Simon & Schuster Inc. (USA) and Scott Ferris Associates (Canada).

ory, both as a feast of ensemble acting and as a warning against prejudice and careless assumption. Valuable points are being made all the way, not only about the jury system but about human nature; while the student dramatist will be dazzled by the way Reginald Rose ensures that we gradually come to know each of the twelve characters so precisely that we would recognize them instantly in the street. Dramatically the only flaw, if it counts as one, is that from the moment one man stands out against an instant vote of guilty, we know that there must be a total reversal: it's the only way to go. One might also admit that the final conversion of the most recalcitrant character is accompanied by a shade too much melodrama. Well, the Greeks overemphasized too; and without this excess we could scarcely feel the catharsis, the immense relief of the final scene, when we emerge from the claustrophobic room into the open air, almost smelling its sweetness after the storm, elated that justice has been done and that the system for once has triumphed over those who would demean it by their petty greeds and jealousies:

> One by one they walk into the rain, each reading with his own maneuvers. One turns up his collar. One pulls down his hat. One holds a newspaper over his head. They begin to move down the steps, in groups and singly now. Juror number eight is alone: He walks into close-up, rain beating his face. He raises his collar, looks around, and then walks off. The others begin to spread out now. Some turning left, some right, some going straight ahead. Camera moves back up, ending with a long shot, through the pelting rain, of the steps and the jurors spreading out silently in all directions, never to see each other again. And finally they are gone, and the rain beats down on the empty steps.

There was a stage version too, which failed to work because we in the audience could not get close enough to the actors' faces and because half of them had to sit with their backs to the audience unless excuses were made to have them stand up and face us. This is a subject for film, and this film is no cheap rip-off shot from the sixth row of the stalls, but a cunningly composed piece of screencraft in which every single shot is calculated to have the fullest possible dramatic impact. Would that Sidney Lumet had approached all his subsequent films with such confidence and care! His direction here is both painstaking and subtle, telling us much about character simply from the way he sets up his shots. There are few long takes: much sharp and exciting work has taken place in the editing rooms. Even in these restricting circumstances the eye is never once allowed to get bored. Helped immeasurably by Boris Kaufman's superior cinematography, the actors make their characters live even when they are only peripherally in shot.

THE CAST

A more able cast could scarcely have been assembled. Henry Fonda, who plays the first doubting juror, number eight, was apparently the driving force behind the production and [throughout his life remained] saddened and puzzled by its failure to make money. It is an archetypal Fonda performance, subtle and caring, yet despite being the catalyst of the drama he seems the least interesting of the group: virtue has the drawback of being sometimes a little dull.

Even without the peg of a name on which to hang their characterizations, the other eleven members of the cast are at least his equal in their claims on our attention:

Number one, the foreman, is Martin Balsam, a small nervous fellow trying not to show how pleased he is at his election. 'Now you gentlemen can handle this any way you want to. I mean, I'm not going to make any rules.'

Number two, John Fiedler, has least to say: a Milquetoast without the courage of his own convictions, until almost by accident he comes out with a clinching piece of observation; before that he has domestic worries on his mind. 'I wonder if they'll let us go home in case we don't finish tonight. I got a boy with mumps.'

Lee J. Cobb has one of the most dominating roles as number three, the loud-mouthed bully who has family reasons for distrusting modern youth and is determined to take out his prejudices on the defendant. 'It's the kids, the way they are nowadays. Listen, when I was his age I used to call my father sir. That's right. Sir! You ever hear a boy call his father that any more?'

The intellectual view is presented by E.G. Marshall as number four. He prides himself on his clear understanding of the facts, and is tough to convince, but not above admitting his mistake. 'I have a reasonable doubt now.'

Jack Klugman as number five is a well-meaning nonentity who constantly tries to pour oil on troubled waters but is roused to anger when it's suggested that slums breed nothing but crime. 'I lived in a slum all my life. I used to play in a back yard that was filled with garbage. Maybe it still smells on me.'

Number six, Edward Binns, is a dull fellow who listens earnestly but always sides with the majority. 'I'm not used to supposing. I'm just a working man. My boss does the supposing.'

Jack Warden makes number seven a harmless slob whose main objective is to get away in time for the baseball game. 'All this yakkin's getting us nowhere. I'm changing my vote to not guilty.'

Fonda as number eight presents the case that defence counsel so obviously failed to prepare. 'Look, this boy's been kicked around all his life. He's had a pretty terrible nineteen years. I think maybe we owe him a few words, that's all.'

Number nine is a frail elderly man, Joseph Sweeney, with a kind of native wisdom and a capacity for anger when ignored. 'If you keep shouting at the top of your lungs . . . I'd like to be a little younger.'

Ed Begley makes number ten an unattractive bigot with a touch of fascist and some irritating mannerisms. 'You can talk till your tongue is draggin' on the floor. The boy is guilty. Period. Know what I mean, my friend?'

Number eleven, George Voskovec, is a European refugee watchmaker, quick to champion the underdog. 'I have always thought that a man was entitled to have unpopular opinions in this country. That is why I came here.'

And number twelve, Robert Webber, is a brainless young advertising executive who prefers doodling to giving the case his full attention. 'It had a lot of interest for me. No dead spots. I tell you, we were lucky to get a murder case. I figured us for a burglary or an assault or something. Those can be the dullest. Say, isn't that the Woolworth building?'

Twelve rounded characterizations, plus the unravelling of a mystery in ninety-odd minutes, is value for money in anybody's language; but as Fonda discovered, the public felt cheated when word of mouth described *Twelve Angry Men* as a film shot in one cheap set. I first encountered it as manager of the Ambassador, Slough. I played it from Monday to Wednesday, one cold week in February. We did moderately with it, and a few patrons commented that it was a film they'd remember; but we trebled the daily income at the end of the week with a double bill of Audie Murphy and Abbott and Costello.

The 1996 London Stage Version Is Timely

Matt Wolf

In 1996, the renowned British playwright and stage director Harold Pinter staged a revival of *Twelve Angry Men* at the Comedy Theatre in London. Reginald Rose produced a special rewrite of the script for the running. The following American review discusses the play's effectiveness and relevance in the era of the O.J. Simpson trial. It also mentions the performances of several well-known British actors (who are unknown to most Americans) playing 1950s American jurors, giving color and life to this revival.

It should come as no surprise to hear that "Twelve Angry Men" is timely, since Reginald Rose's courtroom drama anticipates our own jury-obsessed age by some four decades. The revelation—and a sad one it is—is that the playwright's liberal, humane voice nowadays seems so passe. In Rose's scenario, the (unseen) defendant is deemed guilty largely because he is not white, and it takes all the quiet persistence Juror No. 8 (Kevin Whately) can muster to lay his fellow jurors' bigotry bare.

Come the O.J. era of the 1990s, and an automatic verdict of guilty under the same circumstances would be no more likely than a jury entirely composed of white men. (One could argue, indeed, that a jury today would be as reluctant to find a comparable defendant guilty as the men in the play are to find him innocent.)

But if the social givens of this play have gone, so has the philosophy that underpins it. Its title notwithstanding, "Twelve Angry Men" in 1996 seems a startlingly innocent work in its belief in a fundamental integrity to the legal process that the intervening decades have eroded, perhaps forever.

Excerpted from "Review of *Twelve Angry Men*," by Matt Wolf, *Variety*, May 20–26, 1996. Reprinted with permission from *Variety* magazine.

"Twelve Angry Men" is a riveting social document; that much is clear. And what of it as a play? On that front, Rose's achievement is more muted, though even some occasionally wayward dramaturgy cannot waylay his intentions. As Juror No. 8 accumulates a degree of "reasonable doubt" that makes one wonder how the case ever avoided being thrown out, the author's more pressing point becomes clear. The anger of the title at heart relates not to the 11 jurors who change sides but to the crusading instincts of Whately's lone man of reason who has the courage to acknowledge that "prejudice obscures the truth."

The play is tendentious, even deliberately so, but it is also a narrative of a propulsive sort to explain Rose's triple reworking of it as a 1954 telefilm, an Oscar-nominated movie, and a stage play, the last of which was first seen on the [London] West End in 1964. The jurors aren't individuated characters—their unnamed status tells you as much—and some of their capitulations seem guided more by expediency than dramatic sense: When a snarling Juror 10 (Peter Vaughan, as the most overtly bigoted) changes his verdict just to be done with it, you know how he feels.

How Times Have Changed

Charles Spencer, a theater reviewer for the London news-paper Daily Telegraph, *penned these words in his 1996 review of Harold Pinter's stage revival of* Twelve Angry Men. *Although they were written for a British audience, they also address—with great punch—American issues. Note that in this version of the play, Reginald Rose made the defendant black, not Hispanic.*

With a smouldering and finally explosive performance from Peter Vaughan as the most venomous juror, *Twelve Angry Men* also explores the ugliness of racial prejudice as it becomes clear that the accused youth is black. This bracingly humane play seems to me to be timely in two ways. With more than 3,000 prisoners sweating on death row in the States, it vividly demonstrates the terrible risk of sentencing the wrong man to his death. but it also makes one uneasily aware of how much times have changed. Rose suggests that race could have been a factor in causing a faulty conviction. Nowadays American juries are reluctant to convict blacks for fear of riots. In both cases, justice is the loser.

Charles Spencer, *Daily Telegraph,* April 23, 1996.

Still, there's real dramatic juice in watching the men succumb like so many human dominoes, even if their psychology retains an air of stale '50s psychodrama. (Tony Haygarth's Juror 3 wants a guilty verdict so as to find an outlet for his deep rage towards his own son.) One juror is swung not by anything to do with the teenager on trial but by admiration for Juror 8's nervy outspokenness.

Others sway as bits of evidence—the angle of the lethal switchblade, an eyewitness' vision—are called to question. Still others incriminate themselves with blanket pronouncements they later regret, while British TV star Whately ("Inspector Morse"), inheriting Henry Fonda's screen role, works hard not to look smug.

Eileen Diss' set locks these archetypes in visually symmetrical combat, though the sultry summer's day the play is set on is rarely evoked. (Cheers, however, to Tom Lishman's sound design, which is very recognizably New York.)

The director, Harold Pinter, animates a room of quarreling heads without delivering the wallop he recently brought to another polemical American play, David Mamet's "Oleanna."

And if the American accents often waver, the same could never be said of a playwright whose convictions are that much more stirring in an age, like ours, that has toppled into cynicism.

Updating the Screenplay for the 1997 Remake

Susan King

In 1997, the cable channel Showtime remade the
film *Twelve Angry Men*. In this version, starring two-
time Oscar winner Jack Lemmon, the jury remained
all-male but became racially mixed. Although the
script remained essentially unchanged, Rose updated cultural references, made the racist juror
African American, and added a woman to the cast
(as the judge in the opening sequence). Susan King,
a staff writer for the *Los Angeles Times*, wrote this
film review, which ran in that paper on August 17,
1997, the same day that the remake aired.

Over the past 30 years, William Friedkin has directed such
acclaimed films as "The French Connection," for which he
won the Oscar, "The Exorcist," "The Night They Raided
Minsky's" and "Boys in the Band."

But it's his latest project—a remake of the 1957 classic "12
Angry Men"—that holds a new special place in his heart.

"It was a pure experience working with a great piece of
material with a great cast," Friedkin explains. "Therefore, it
is probably the most memorable experience I've ever had."

"12 Angry Men" . . . deals with jurors deliberating a death-
penalty case in which a young Latino man is accused of
murder.

The jury deciding the verdict represents all walks of life.
Juror No. 10 (Mykelti Williamson) is an outspoken bigot who
was kicked out of the Nation of Islam. Juror No. 4 (Armin
Mueller-Stahl) is a proper stockbroker. Juror No. 9 (Hume
Cronyn) is an elderly man with health problems. Juror No.
11 (Edward James Olmos) is a European watchmaker who
believes in justice. Juror No. 2 (Ossie Davis) is a bank clerk.
Juror No. 3 (George C. Scott) is full of rage and venom.

Excerpted from "In the Jury Room," by Susan King, *Los Angeles Times*, August 17, 1997.
Reprinted with permission from the *Los Angeles Times*.

From the outset, 11 of the jurors believe the youth should be convicted. But well-dressed Juror No. 8 (Jack Lemmon) isn't sure of the boy's guilt. His doubt fuels the drama.

COMPARING THE VERSIONS

Penned by Reginald Rose, "12 Angry Men" originally debuted to great acclaim as a live TV drama in 1954 on CBS' "Studio One." The teleplay, which won an Emmy Award that year, starred Robert Cummings as Juror No. 8 and Franchot Tone as No. 3. Three years later, Rose adapted "Men" for the big screen, with Henry Fonda as No. 8 and Lee J. Cobb as No. 3. Directed by Sidney Lumet, the film was nominated for an Academy Award for best picture of the year.

"I like '12 Angry Men,'" says Rose. "It has served me well."

Rose came up with the idea for the teleplay after serving on a jury in 1954. "It was so formal back then," he says. "I was so impressed. I had never been in a courtroom before. There was a terrible battle in the jury room over the verdict. We argued and screamed for 8 hours. It was 12 white men, which was what most juries were then. I said [to myself], 'What a wonderful situation for a one-hour television play that takes place in real time.' I invented the case and I invented the characters."

For the remake, Friedkin rehearsed his cast for eight days and then shot the movie in sequence in just two weeks. "It was all hand-held cameras—two, sometimes only one. . . . I wanted a lot of spontaneity. I wasn't going for perfection; I was going for realism."

Lemmon says making the movie was exciting for the cast, which also included Courtney B. Vance, William Petersen, Dorian Harewood, Tony Danza and James Gandolfini. "We loved everybody else in the cast as actors," he explains. "Even if you weren't in the shot, everybody was on the set watching."

The two-time Oscar winner was a fan of the 1957 Lumet film, but took a completely different approach to playing No. 8 than Fonda did. "I felt from the very beginning in Hank's portrayal that [he felt the kid was not guilty]," Lemmon says. "This is the way he felt and he knew what he had to try to do. Whereas [in my interpretation], I didn't honestly know [if he was innocent]."

Friedkin came up with the idea of remaking "Men" during the height of the O.J. Simpson trial, [in 1995] after showing the film to his then-12-year-old son and his friends, who wanted to know more about the justice system.

"At that time," he says, "I was looking at five or six lame scripts that had been offered me, wondering why they don't write them like this anymore. I looked at this and said, 'I bet I could put together a really great cast and do this today.'"

Friedkin talked with Rose about perhaps adding women to the piece.

THE NEW JURY IN THE 1997 REMAKE OF *TWELVE ANGRY MEN*

In this excerpt from a 1997 Newsday *film review, Reginald Rose discusses the addition of African American actors to the jury for the Showtime remake of* Twelve Angry Men.

Four of [director William] Friedkin's *Angry Men* are African-American. "I went to Reginald Rose," the director said at the [1997] TV critics' press tour, "and said, I'd like to try and put this together with a really fine cast. And I'm not going to pay any attention to what color these guys are." The only script change required was when "[African-American actor] Mykelti [Williamson, who plays the bigoted Juror #10] came in with the idea of doing his guy as a sort of busted Nation of Islam guy," recalled Friedkin. "How many times do you see a black racist portrayed?"

Diane Werts, "Glued to the Tube," *Newsday*, August 12, 1997.

"Having women, you can't call it '12 Angry Men,'" Rose says.

Plus, Rose would have had to have done major rewrites to the script, instead of just updating cultural references and adding a few lines about No. 10's association with the Nation of Islam.

(Friedkin, though, did manage to cast a woman in "Men." Mary McDonell plays the judge in the opening sequence.)

"This is really about guys venting at each other," Friedkin says. "I wanted to keep the title and the piece as it was. The jury is a metaphor for the behavior of men."

Rose and Friedkin did agree that the jury should be racially mixed. The most interesting casting choice was to have an African American play the juror whose bigotry toward the Latino defendant shows through. "You never see a member of a minority playing a racist," Friedkin says.

"I thought making Mykelti a bigot was absolutely fascinating," Lemmon adds.

But the role took its toll on Williamson.

"It was the hardest thing I ever had to do," he says. "I figured it would be like any other job: You would do your research, really lock on your character and surrender yourself to the character. But I had no idea how ugly of an environment I would have to exist in in order to bring the reality of the character onto the screen."

Williamson was besieged daily with bad headaches. "I didn't like the character," he explains. "I had a hard time looking people in the eye when I was working because I had all of these racist thoughts in my head. I was so ashamed of myself. The night after we wrapped, I went home, had a glass of wine and cried [for] over an hour. I was so ashamed. I hope my Latino brothers and sisters understand that it is a performance only, nothing more than that."

CHAPTER 4

Jury Behavior in Real Life

READINGS ON
TWELVE ANGRY MEN

How Jurors Deliberate and Reach Verdicts

Melvyn Bernard Zerman

When a jury is forced to bring itself to a unanimous (or near unanimous) decision, it is the ultimate expression of the democratic process. In the following article, author Melvyn Bernard Zerman, who has written extensively on the American jury system, describes what a person can expect as a juror, from as basic as what a typical jury room looks like to the types of jury foremen and *de facto* jury leadership. He goes on to explain that, despite the portrayals in *Twelve Angry Men*, most real-life juries come to agreement right away or the minority position gives way to the majority position.

Some juries never agree on a verdict at all. Their members spend hours and then days in reasoned discussion, angry debate, and desperate pleading. They exchange words, ideas, experiences, and invective. They admit their doubts, their prejudices, their fears—and, finally, their defeat. They are, it is said, "at an impasse" and "hopelessly deadlocked."

Agreeing only to disagree, they transmit this decision to the court, perhaps with reluctance, probably with disappointment, but mostly in exhaustion and relief. The judge—impatient, frustrated, irate—has no choice but to acknowledge their failure, particularly if he has refused to accept it earlier and again and again has sent them back to continue their deliberations. He is faced now with what is known as a hung jury. Quite possibly from his point of view and that of the prosecutor—though not necessarily that of the defense—the time, the effort, and the money spent on trying the case have been wasted. But if these twelve people could not reach a verdict perhaps another group of twelve can. And so the whole procedure may start again.

Excerpted from *Beyond a Reasonable Doubt: Inside the American Jury System*, by Melvyn B. Zerman (New York: Thomas Y. Crowell, 1981). Copyright ©1988 by Melvyn B. Zerman. Reprinted with permission from the author.

The forces that produce a hung jury are at work in every jury room—just as strong, just as active, and potentially just as divisive. But when they are brought under control, and they usually are—only 6 percent of all criminal trials end with a hung jury—the result, at least on the surface, is quite splendid: twelve people, thrown together by chance, have exercised their free will, their knowledge, and their intelligence to arrive unanimously at a crucial decision. Truly, we have here the ultimate expression of the democratic process.

Or do we? What actually happens in a jury room is usually neither as torturous as the struggle that ends in a hung jury nor as glorious as the ideal envisioned by those who gave us the jury system. The realities of jury behavior can be traced to nothing more or less than human nature; while, obviously, these realities are of vital interest to lawyers, political scientists, and even historians, they are equally the province of psychologists.

Since no "outsider" is ever allowed to observe or overhear what goes on in a jury room, studies of jury behavior are based for the most part on after-trial interviews with jurors, or on simulated juries made up of college students or of people challenged during a *voir dire* [the jury selection process]. Neither approach is totally satisfactory because neither can precisely reconstruct the way an actual jury functions: ex-jurors are not likely to recall everything they experienced of interest and importance, and simulated juries are free of that most burdensome responsibility of real juries, the knowledge that their verdicts will have serious consequences.

These weaknesses notwithstanding, studies of how juries deliberate are both fascinating and valuable and from them many generalizations can be drawn. . . . Let's describe where it all happens.

[Imagine that you are a juror.] As you retire to deliberate, you return to the room where no doubt you have already spent a good deal of waiting time. It is a place of work, not of relaxation, and as such it is sparsely furnished and strictly functional. Dominated by a large table, it contains little else besides twelve reasonably comfortable chairs, some ashtrays, perhaps a water pitcher and glasses. If the room has windows—and it may not—don't expect a view or access to fresh air. The glass will be opaque or crisscrossed with steel mesh and the windows will be sealed and perhaps even barred. There will be no way for you to signal to anyone outside. And forget about leaving early. The door to the room is locked from the outside and can be opened only by the court officer who stands constant guard in the hallway. Once the jury has retired to deliberate, no one is allowed to enter or leave the jury room except under the most extraordinary circumstances (the sudden illness of a juror, for example), and the jurors may move only en masse to return to the courtroom or to go to a restaurant or hotel. There is a lavatory off the jury room—the only place where a juror can find solitude and the only place where two or three jurors can find a retreat from the rest of the group. In other words, the bathroom may, on occasion, be used for a purpose for which it was not designed.

Choosing a Leader

Once you are settled in the jury room, you may be eager or hesitant to begin deliberations, but in either case the forces that govern all group decision making—unstated, instinctive—immediately come into play; the first of these is the need for leadership.

In some states, like New York, the *nominal* leader is already known in that the first juror chosen in the *voir dire* is automatically the foreman or forewoman of the jury. Whether this person then becomes the *actual* leader of the deliberations depends upon several factors: his or her personality and experience in group leadership, the personalities of other members of the jury, and, if the nominal leader has already reached an opinion as to the defendant's guilt, how firmly he or she holds that view.

Certainly, the fact that a person has been designated foreman or forewoman and is acknowledged as such during the course of the trial provides him or her with a definite advantage in assuming real leadership. Once in the jury room, the eleven other jurors will expect that person to sit at the head of the table and will look to him or her to direct the initial discussion. This is a crucial moment in determining who will be the real leader of the deliberations and, perhaps, even in determining the jury's final verdict. Let us imagine three very different foremen and forewomen and their opening comments:

No. 1: "I've never served on a jury before and I don't know much about it, but I guess we should start by taking a vote."

No. 2: "If no one has any objection, I think we should go around the table so that each of us can say what he or she thinks."

No. 3: "Okay, so you should know where I stand, let me tell you that I think this joker is guilty from the word go. Now if anybody disagrees with me, let's hear it."

Foreman No. 1 is at best a reluctant leader. He begins by confessing his inadequacy and his first, rather tentative decision—to take a vote—actually serves to delay the time when he must assert himself. Beginning with a poll of the jurors, which is quite common in deliberations, provides among other benefits an immediate indication of the challenge ahead. After the outcome of the vote is known, Foreman No. 1 may decide that he can effectively take charge, but the chances are good that he will either deliberately relinquish his power to someone else or find his power gradually eroding as other more forceful jurors take command of the discussion. He will remain the only person through whom the other jurors, individually and collectively, may communicate with the court, and he will, of course, have the honor of publicly announcing the jury's verdict, but otherwise he will be no more than one of the group.

Forewoman No. 2 is a reasonable, thoughtful type—perhaps a natural leader, perhaps not. She rejects the easy choice of a quick vote in favor of an approach that will yield richer material for discussion and, at the same time, suggest the range of juror sentiment almost as clearly as polling will. It is unlikely that anyone will object to her around-the-table method although some jurors may elect to pass when it is their turn to speak. In any case, Forewoman No. 2 has demonstrated important leadership qualities in her opening statement. At this point, unless she is totally undecided about the verdict while most of the other jurors are in full agreement, she will probably be forewoman in more than name only.

Foreman No. 3, who may well have been a top sergeant in the army, is a "born leader." Perhaps not the best kind of leader for jury deliberations (or anything else), he is nonetheless a take-charge kind of person who immediately identifies himself as such, thereby challenging anyone to question his authority. Indeed, in his opening statement he is almost daring his fellow jurors to disagree with him. It is to be hoped that not everyone will be intimidated. But intimidation is one way of asserting leadership, and Foreman No. 3 uses it to try to solidify a position he originally attained purely by chance. He is foreman. Anybody want to make something out of it? Perhaps someone will.

Merely conferring the title of Foreman or Forewoman on someone does not then guarantee that that person will be the leader of the jury. In effect, the role must be earned by seizing control of circumstances. This can be true even when the foreman or forewoman is chosen by the more prevalent method of having the jurors select their own leader. If the jurors do not know one another very well—if the trial has been short or has moved very quickly—they have little or no basis on which to make a choice. Indeed, many juries finesse the issue by simply drawing lots. Obviously, a foreman chosen in this way is hardly more secure in his role than a first-juror foreman. The least vulnerable foreman is the person who wins the most votes in an election among those who feel they know him. Of course, the closer the balloting, the shakier his position. But, regardless of how the vote divides or how solid are the grounds on which the jurors make their choice, the election procedure automatically confers a legitimacy that a leader selected in any other way must work to—and may never—achieve.

THE DELIBERATIONS BEGIN

With a leader in place, at least temporarily, the jurors begin their deliberations. Let's consider first a not-so-rare occurrence—reaching unanimity of opinion on the first go-around, be it by vote or organized discussion. Immediate and complete agreement among jurors happens more frequently than you might think—31 percent of the time, it is estimated. The jury in the Lizzie Borden trial was a dramatic illustration of the phenomenon—and for people who wish to avoid conflict and controversy and get home early, too—which probably means most of us—it is a cherished blessing. What brings it about?

Primarily, the weight of the state's evidence. There *are* open-and-shut cases, and more often they are shut on the guilty side: 19 percent of immediate verdicts are for conviction, 12 percent for acquittal. Moreover, when an effective attack by the prosecution is aimed at an unsympathetic defendant—someone who, whether he or she takes the stand or not, inspires suspicion, dislike, and distrust—you have a situation where twelve people can easily come to the same negative conclusion.

Conversely, a weak case by the prosecution can be further undermined by an attractive defendant—not merely physically attractive, although that certainly helps, but seemingly honest, clean-cut (which is why defense attorneys insist that their clients be well-groomed in the courtroom even if their normal mode of dress and hair style tends to the flamboyant), gentle, and—innocent. A quick not-guilty verdict may also be prompted by a flood of compassion for the defendant. Remember the defense summation in which the accused becomes the victim: "My client has suffered enough." When jurors can be made to see the defendant in an inordinately sympathetic light, and particularly when the crime with which he or she is charged is not regarded as terribly serious (shoplifting, for example) and the state's case is somewhat vulnerable, the chances are good that no one will vote for conviction. Acquittals like these almost always rest on the jurors' shared belief that, whatever the person may have done in the past, he or she is not likely to commit a crime in the future. Like Jesus in the *Book of John,* the jury is saying, "Neither do I condemn thee: go, and sin no more."

MOST JURIES DISAGREE

But it would be naive to enter a jury room expecting speedy agreement among a group of twelve very different individuals. Research has shown that even when jurors at the outset of their deliberations find themselves in substantial accord, they feel an obligation to discuss the case at some length. A jury that returns a verdict in less than an hour probably had no conflicts to resolve but enjoyed a thorough rehash of the trial.

Most juries, of course, do experience disagreement. Usually it emerges quite early and, at once, lines are drawn. People choose sides, leaving perhaps a pool of players, "the undecideds," who will later join one team or the other. But although the contest between the "guilties" and the "not-guilties" will take shape rather rapidly, it is difficult to know how long the game will last. However, if one side is much stronger in numbers than the other, it is fairly easy to predict the final outcome.

Common sense tells us that a division of votes that borders on unanimity—that is, eleven to one—means that the eleven are sure to triumph. In spite of such fictions as *Twelve*

Angry Men (in which a single juror manages, after hours of dramatic confrontation, to twist and batter his colleagues around to his view), the position of a person who *from the beginning* stands apart as a lonely "holdout" is virtually insupportable. One of the fundamental rules of group behavior—and a rule that is so essential to the efficient discharge of a jury's duty that without it the very system probably could not exist—is that people want to identify with and be part of the majority.

THE JURY SYSTEM WORKS

Despite the cynics of the American jury system, research shows that in most cases judges agree with juries' findings, pointing to the conclusion that juries make sound decisions.

Critics have argued that the jury system fails on many grounds, primarily because juries are judged to be incompetent, prejudiced, and unreliable. Our best research refutes those claims. The data from hundreds of jury trials, empirical studies, jury simulations, and archival searches suggest that juries are not incompetent. There are instances when judges and juries have disagreed, but these disagreements are more often attributable to factors other than juror incompetence. In those cases where juries deviate from what the judge would have decided, that deviation usually results from the jury's different sense of justice rather than from jury incompetence.

Allen J. Hart, "Jury Psychology," in V.S. Ramachandran, *Encyclopedia of Human Behavior*, 1994.

It takes great personal courage and uncommonly strong conviction for anyone to hold to an unpopular view, and the degree of courage and conviction required is almost directly proportional to the unpopularity of that view. When it can be expressed as one against eleven, the pressure felt by the holdout—from the rest of the group and, more important, from within himself—will eventually become too painful to tolerate. The majority assumes that it is right if only because it *is* the majority, and a lopsided one at that; therefore, the odds against its losing power—that is, members—are staggering. Not only will the holdout be unable to win adherents to his side, he will eventually become the target of a relentless attack. From all around the table jurors will be urging him to remember certain pieces of evidence, reminding him of the testimony of one witness or another, demanding that he answer a variety of pointed questions, and—depending on how long it takes for him to succumb—begging him to be reasonable and assailing him for being pigheaded. Few of us could sustain such an onslaught for very long; almost inevitably the holdout will give in. Making his concession immeasurably easier will be one incontrovertible fact: eleven other people, many of whom must be as intelligent as he, heard the same testimony and saw the same evidence and came to a common conclusion. Isn't it likely, therefore, that their verdict and not his is the correct one?

Most juries that are at first divided much more evenly than eleven to one eventually reach a stage in deliberations when they, too, face a single holdout. In such situations much of the above applies, but a juror who at one time had allies seems to gain tenacity from that support even after it has vanished. He is much more likely to remain a minority of one forever—that is, until the court accepts a hung jury. In union there is strength, and somehow when *two* jurors share the unpopular position, their power is more than twice as great as that of the lonely holdout. Thus, a ten to two vote at the outset is much closer to a nine to three or an eight to four vote in its effect upon the course and duration of the jury's debate.

"Debate"—the very word suggests two sides that are more or less evenly matched, and for a jury's deliberations to be thought of as a debate we must assume that the weak side consists of at least two people. Given that, of one thing these minority jurors can be sure: at some point they will be put on the defensive. For a second fundamental rule of jury behavior is that the minority must eventually try to justify its position to the majority. A third rule is that the greater the number of people in the minority, the easier it will be for them to defend their position successfully. But a well-documented finding considerably dilutes the importance of both these rules; in most cases a jury's first ballot—assuming, of course, that it is not a tie—indicates what the final verdict will be. Even if, allowing for some "undecideds," one side takes the initial lead by merely a single vote, that side will probably prevail in the end. . . .

Cut Off from the World

In one important sense every jury is sequestered: for as long as it takes them to reach a verdict, the twelve people are imprisoned in a room that is totally cut off from the outside world. Deprived of the contacts, relationships, and activities that give substance to their everyday lives, they are forced to create together a new, if temporary, world, one in which they are the only inhabitants, twelve chairs and a table the only furnishings, and blank walls the only landscape. But into this world rush all sorts of invisible agents—the experiences, perceptions, and attitudes accumulated over a dozen disparate lifetimes and a comparatively few shared hours. It is impossible to predict how these varying factors will clash or correspond, what sparks will be struck, which paths will converge. In the small world of the jury room the possibilities of conflict, compromise, and accommodation are as infinite as are the ways of human behavior in the world outside the courthouse.

We have tried in this article to identify and illustrate some principles and practices that are common to jury deliberations. If space allowed we could have analyzed jury deliberations in trial after trial, reducing hours of discussion and debate to a handful of key developments, isolating the people and the pronouncements that, seen in retrospect, hastened the trend or turned the tide toward one verdict or another. But all our knowledge of the past can give us no certainty for the future, for every jury creates a new world of its own. Listen to a man who has just rejoined the world outside:

> I knew the defendant was guilty but I didn't know how or why I knew. I sensed it, that's all; I sensed it. The lawyers were no help at all. You wouldn't believe how unevenly matched they were. If they'd been in a boxing ring, the referee would have stopped the fight a minute into the first round. The D.A. was a total incompetent. I guess he was inexperienced—he seemed pretty young—and he was almost inarticulate. He kept repeating himself and missing opportunities to make points. He didn't even try to build up the testimony that could have helped him, and he was like struck dumb and powerless against the witnesses who hurt him. I'm sure you can tell I've served on juries before and let me say this guy was the pits—the absolute bottom.

> To make matters worse, he was up against a defense attorney who was spectacular—really, a legal virtuoso. Of course, there was no way he could prove this guy was innocent but that's not the name of the game anyhow. He just ripped the state's case to shreds. The D.A.'s expert witnesses left the stand looking like embarrassed amateurs. The eyewitnesses might just as well have been blind when that lawyer got

through with them. I'm telling you, when the D.A. rested his case, it was like burying a bunch of dust. Unbelievable. But still I *knew* the guy was guilty. I *sensed* that he was guilty. But convincing the other jurors of that—forget it.

There was one woman who agreed with me, and it was the two of us against the mob. Almost from the moment we walked in the jury room, and certainly after the first vote, the ten of them were shouting at us to explain why we wanted to convict and, dammit, we had no answer. And they would trot out this argument and that argument and all I could say was, "The lawyer made you see it that way. He twisted the testimony around." And then all of a sudden I remembered. It must have been lodged in my unconscious all the time and that's why I sensed he was guilty. Nothing to do with any witnesses or testimony or evidence or lawyers or judge. Nothing to do with any prejudices or even gut feelings. I was just sitting there picturing the defendant and then it hit me. There was never a moment when two armed cops weren't standing next to him.

I've served on three criminal cases—one of them for murder—and I never saw that before. This guy was up for armed robbery. Why did he need that honor guard? I asked the ten jurors that. About half of them had served on a criminal case before and they all admitted that they'd never seen a defendant guarded that way. Well, that broke the ice. We all started to see through the lawyer's tactics. It took a while but we convicted. Afterwards we found out that the guy was an escaped con, serving a term for manslaughter. That's why he had those cops with him all the time: his own personal cops. They never said a word but they nailed him all right.

CHRONOLOGY

DECEMBER 10, 1920

Reginald Rose is born in New York City, to William and Alice (Obendorfer) Rose.

1929

The U.S. stock market crashes in October. Joseph Stalin becomes the leader of the Soviet Union.

NOVEMBER 1, 1932

Franklin D. Roosevelt is elected for his first term as the thirty-second president of the United States; following his inauguration, work begins on the New Deal to combat the Great Depression.

NOVEMBER 3, 1936

President Roosevelt is elected to his second term.

SUMMER 1939

Television technology makes its unofficial public debut at the New York World's Fair; RCA chairman David Sarnoff opens the fair by addressing the public through television, as does President Roosevelt, becoming the first president to appear on TV. The first regular American television broadcasts begin this year, only to be suspended two years later as a result of World War II.

SEPTEMBER 1, 1939

Adolf Hitler's forces invade Poland, marking the start of World War II.

NOVEMBER 5, 1940

President Roosevelt is elected to his third term.

1941–1945

The Southern California Communist Party membership reaches a wartime high of four thousand.

DECEMBER 7, 1941

Japan bombs Pearl Harbor. The U.S. Congress declares war the following day.

1942–1946

Reginald Rose serves in the U.S. Army Quartermaster Corps as an enlisted man and then as an officer, retiring as a first lieutenant.

1943

Rose marries Barbara Langbart; four sons will be born of this marriage.

NOVEMBER 7, 1944

President Roosevelt is elected to his fourth term.

APRIL 12, 1945

President Roosevelt dies in office; Harry S. Truman becomes the thirty-third president of the United States.

MAY 8, 1945

President Truman declares Victory-in-Europe Day (VE Day).

SEPTEMBER 2, 1945

World War II ends with the surrender of Japan, following the dropping of atomic bombs on Hiroshima and Nagasaki in August.

FALL 1945

Post–WWII television broadcasts begin. By the end of World War II, the USSR, under Joseph Stalin, has expanded its empire to include Poland, Ukraine, Belorussia, portions of Finland, Latvia, Lithuania, Estonia, Romania and Moldavia, East Germany, parts of China and Japan, Hungary, Bulgaria, Yugoslavia, and Albania; Czechoslovakia will be added in 1948.

1947

The United States adopts a policy of containment toward the Soviet Union, proposing to stop further Soviet territorial expansion.

MARCH 1947

U.S. representative John Rankin (D-Miss.), a member of the House Un-American Activities Committee (HUAC), calls for a cleansing of the film industry. Some HUAC members, such as Chairman J. Parnell Thomas, are concerned with possible "Communist propaganda" being injected into Hollywood movies.

OCTOBER 1947

The HUAC holds hearings investigating communism in motion pictures. It subpoenas forty-one witnesses, nineteen of whom loudly and belligerently declare themselves to be "unfriendly." Eleven of those unfriendly witnesses are called, ten of whom are charged the following November with contempt of Congress, becoming the Hollywood Ten.

NOVEMBER 24, 1947

Fifty Hollywood executives meet at the Waldorf-Astoria Hotel in New York City to devise a way to avoid looking like they are harboring Communists. An industry blacklist is born, lasting until the 1960s.

NOVEMBER 3, 1948

President Truman is elected to a second term.

NOVEMBER 7, 1948

CBS's *Studio One* airs its first television broadcast. (It had been a radio show since spring 1947.)

OCTOBER 1, 1949

Chinese leader Mao Tse-tung's Red Army gains control of China. The United States refuses to recognize the new Chinese government; instead it adopts a policy of containment toward China similar to that in place toward the Soviet Union.

FEBRUARY 9, 1950

Senator Joseph R. McCarthy (R-Wisc.) publicly charges that there are 205 unnamed Communists working in the U.S. State Department.

APRIL 1950

The Supreme Court declines to hear the appeals of the Hollywood Ten, leaving their conviction standing; all ten are fined $1,000 and serve time in prison.

MARCH 21, 1951

The HUAC begins a second round of hearings regarding Communist influence and influencers in the entertainment industry. These hearings result in more than two hundred individuals being named as Communists or Communist sympathizers. Hundreds of individuals are added to the industry blacklist.

AUGUST 9, 1951

Senator McCarthy publicly names twenty-six members of the U.S. State Department whom he suspects of disloyalty.

DECEMBER 1951

Rose's first original television play, "The Bus to Nowhere," airs on CBS's *Out There*.

1952

The Federal Communications Commission lifts its freeze on issuing new broadcast licenses, which had been in place since 1948; the TV industry is reinvigorated.

NOVEMBER 7, 1952

Dwight D. Eisenhower is elected to his first term as the thirty-fourth president of the United States. Outspoken anti-Communist Joseph McCarthy is elected to the U.S. Senate for his second term; he is named the chairman of the Senate Subcommittee on Investigations.

1953

Fifty-five percent of all American households own at least one television set.

MARCH 5, 1953

Soviet leader Joseph Stalin dies in office.

NOVEMBER 1953

Rose writes his first hour-long original drama, "The Remarkable Incident at Carson Corners," to be aired in 1954 on CBS's *Studio One*.

MARCH 15, 1954

"Thunder on Sycamore Street" premieres on *Studio One*.

APRIL 22–JUNE 17, 1954

The McCarthy-Army hearings are conducted following McCarthy's charge that Secretary of the Army Robert Stevens and the U.S. Army are concealing foreign espionage activities and the Army's countercharge of impropriety by McCarthy. The hearings last for thirty-six days and are broadcast to an estimated 20 million viewers.

SEPTEMBER 20, 1954

"Twelve Angry Men" premieres on CBS's *Studio One*.

SEPTEMBER 27, 1954

U.S. Senate Select Committee recommends the censure of Senator McCarthy for contempt of the Senate Privileges and Elections Committee.

DECEMBER 2, 1954

The Senate votes to condemn Senator McCarthy.

1955

The 1954 broadcast of "Twelve Angry Men" wins three Emmy Awards (Best Written Dramatic Material, Best Director, and Best Performance by an Actor in Drama) and a Writers Guild of America Laurel Award. Sixty-seven percent of all American households have at least one television set.

1956

Rose's book *Six Television Plays,* which contains the script to "Twelve Angry Men," is published.

NOVEMBER 6, 1956

President Eisenhower is elected to a second term.

APRIL 18, 1957

The film *Twelve Angry Men,* starring Henry Fonda, opens at Capitol Theater in New York City; it closes after a week, a commercial failure.

MAY 2, 1957

Joseph McCarthy dies of a severe attack of hepatitis.

OCTOBER 4, 1957

Sputnik I, the world's first man-made satellite, is launched by the Soviet Union; it initiates the space race between the USSR and the United States and has enormous and fearful military implications for the United States.

MARCH 26, 1958

The Motion Picture Academy Awards for 1957 are presented. *Twelve Angry Men* is nominated for three awards (Best Picture, Best Director, and Best Writing for a Screenplay Based on Another Medium), but it does not win any.

SEPTEMBER 29, 1958

Studio One airs its last television broadcast.

NOVEMBER 1, 1960

John F. Kennedy is elected the thirty-fifth president of the United States.

1961–1965

Rose writes for the television series *The Defenders* (CBS).

1963

Rose marries for a second time, to Ellen McLaughlin; two sons will be born of this marriage.

1972

Rose's book *The Thomas Book* is published.

APRIL 17, 1997

Twelve Angry Men, with an updated script by Rose, is re-made and broadcast on the cable channel Showtime; it includes an all-star cast led by Jack Lemmon, George C. Scott, and Hume Cronyn.

For Further Research

Works by Reginald Rose

Books

Six Television Plays. New York: Simon & Schuster, 1956.

The Thomas Book. New York: Harcourt, Brace, Jovanovich, 1972.

Films

Crime in the Streets, 1956.

Dino, 1957.

Twelve Angry Men (also coproduced), 1957.

Man of the West, 1958.

The Man in the Net, 1958.

Baxter! 1972.

Somebody Killed Her Husband, 1978.

The Wild Geese, 1978.

The Sea Wolves, 1980.

Whose Life Is It, Anyway? (with Brian Clark), 1981.

The Final Option, 1983.

The Wild Geese II, 1985.

Made-for-Television Movies

The Rules of Marriage, 1982.

My Two Loves (with Rita Mae Brown), 1986.

Twelve Angry Men, 1997.

The Defenders: Choice of Evils, 1998.

Stage

Black Monday (first produced off-Broadway at Vandam Theater, New York City), 1962.

Twelve Angry Men (first produced at Queen's Playhouse, London, England), 1964.

The Porcelain Year (produced at Locust Street Theatre, Philadelphia; then Shubert Theatre, New Haven Connecticut), 1965.

Dear Friends (first produced in Edinburgh, Scotland), 1968.

This Agony, This Triumph (first produced in California), 1972.

Television Series

Philco Television Playhouse-Goodyear Playhouse, 1948–1955.

Studio One, 1948–1955.

Out There, 1951.

Elgin Hour, 1954–1955.

The Alcoa Hour-Goodyear Playhouse, 1955–1957.

Playhouse 90, 1956–1961.

Sunday Showcase, 1959–1960.

The Defenders (creator and writer), 1961–1965.

CBS Playhouse, 1967.

The Zoo Gang (creator and writer), 1975.

The Four of Us (pilot), 1977.

Television Miniseries

Studs Lonigan, 1979.

Escape from Sobibor, 1987.

FOR FURTHER RESEARCH ON *TWELVE ANGRY MEN* AND THE PEOPLE WHO MADE IT

Jonathan Baumbach, "Twelve Angry Men," *Film Culture*, 1957.

Peter Biskind, *Seeing Is Believing.* New York: Pantheon Books, 1983.

Stephen E. Bowles, *Sidney Lumet: A Guide to References and Resources.* Boston: G.K. Hall, 1979.

Frank R. Cunningham, *Sidney Lumet: Film and Literary Vision*. Lexington: University Press of Kentucky, 1991.

Alan Dershowitz, "Legal Eagles," *American Film Magazine*, November 1986.

James J. Desmarais, "Twelve Angry Men," *Magill's Survey of Cinema, English Language Films*, vol. 4. Englewood Cliffs, NJ: Salem Press, 1980.

Kevin Dowler, "Reginald Rose," in Horace Newcomb, ed., *Encyclopedia of Television*. Chicago and London: Fitzroy Dearborn, 1997.

Henry Fonda, as told to Howard Teichmann, *Fonda: My Life*. New York and Scarborough, Ontario: New American Library, 1981.

"Good Men and True and All Angry," *Life Magazine*, April 22, 1957.

Leslie Halliwell, "Twelve Angry Men," *Halliwell's Hundred*. New York: Charles Scribner's Sons, 1982.

Thomas J. Harris, *Courtroom's Finest Hour in American Cinema*. Metuchen, NJ, and London: Scarecrow Press, 1987.

Ned E. Hoopes, introduction, *Great Television Plays*. New York: Dell, 1969.

Jason J. Jacobs, "Studio One," in Horace Newcomb, ed., *Encyclopedia of Television*. Chicago and London: Fitzroy Dearborn, 1997.

Carola Kaplan, "Reginald Rose," in Robert E. Morseberger, Stephen O. Lesser, and Randall Clark, eds., *Dictionary of Literary Biography: American Screenwriters*. Detroit, MI: Bruccoli Clark, 1984.

Boris Kaufman, "Filming *Twelve Angry Men* on a Single Set," *American Cinematographer*, December 1956.

William I. Kaufman, ed., *Great Television Plays*. New York: Dell, 1969.

Jeff Kisseloff, *The Box: An Oral History of Television, 1920–1961*. New York: Viking, 1995.

Sidney Lumet, *Making Movies*. New York: Alfred A. Knopf, 1995.

Henry F. Nardone, "Using the Film *12 Angry Men* to Teach Critical Thinking" in F.H. Eemeren, R. Grootenndorst, A. Blair and C. Willards, (eds.) *Proceedings of the 3rd Inter-*

national Conference on Argumentation. The Netherlands: International Centre for the Study of Argumentation, 1995.

Rex Polier, "Reflections on TV's Golden Age," *Los Angeles Times,* January 1, 1982.

Russell F. Proctor II, "Do the Ends Justify the Means?: Thinking Critically About *Twelve Angry Men,*" April 14, 1991.

———, "Teaching Group Communication With Feature Films," paper presented at the Annual Meeting of the Speech Communication Association (77th, Atlanta, GA, October 31–November 3, 1991).

Eleanor Roosevelt, *My Day: First Lady of the World,* ed., David Elmblidge, vol. 3. New York: Pharos Books, 1991.

Reginald Rose, "The Trying Talesmen," *New York Times,* April 7, 1957.

David Burnell Smith, "Reel Justice: The Movies' View of the American Legal System," University of Nevada, Reno, 1995.

Robert Strauss, "The Star Never Showed Up . . . and Other Memories of Live TV," *Newsday,* 1997.

Nicholas Thomas, *International Dictionary of Films and Filmmakers,* 2nd edition, 1990.

Tony Thomas, *The Films of Henry Fonda.* Secaucus, NJ: Citadel Press, 1983.

Susan M. Trosky, ed., *Contemporary Authors.* Detroit, MI: Gale Research, 1994.

François Truffaut, *The Films in My Life,* trans. Leonard Mayhew. New York: Simon & Schuster, 1978.

ORIGINAL REVIEWS OF THE FILM
TWELVE ANGRY MEN (1957)

Hollis Alpert, "12 Angry Men," *Saturday Review,* April 20, 1957.

Philip T. Hartung, "The Screen: Judicial and Prejudicial," *Commonweal,* April 19, 1957.

Ronald Holloway, "12 Angry Men," *Variety,* February 27, 1957.

"12 Angry Men," *America,* April 1957.

"Twelve Angry Men," *Time,* April 29, 1957.

A.H. Weiler, "Citizens Under Stress," *New York Times,* April 21, 1957.

———, "12 Angry Men," *New York Times*, April 15, 1957.

ORIGINAL REVIEWS OF THE PLAY
TWELVE ANGRY MEN **(1996)**

Will Eaves, "Everybody's a Lawyer!" *Times Literary Supplement*, May 17, 1996.

Charles Spencer, "Twelve Angry Men," *Daily Telegraph*, April 23, 1996.

Matt Wolf, "Twelve Angry Men," *Variety*, May 20–26, 1996.

ORIGINAL REVIEWS OF THE TV MOVIE
TWELVE ANGRY MEN **(1997)**

Caryn James, "For These Angry Jurors, the Judge Is a Woman," *New York Times*, August 16, 1997.

Susan King, "In the Jury Room," *Los Angeles Times*, August 17, 1997.

Mike Lipton, "12 Angry Men," *People Magazine*, August 18, 1997.

Tony Scott, "12 Angry Men," *Variety*, August 11, 1997.

Susan Stewart, "12 Angry Men," *TV Guide*, August 16, 1997.

Diane Werts, "Glued to the Tube/Twelve New Angry Men Remake Is Part of a Return to Provocative Days," *Newsday*, August 12, 1997.

ORIGINAL REVIEWS OF THE TV SHOW
TWELVE ANGRY MEN **(1954)**

Leonard Traube, "Studio One," *Variety*, September 22, 1954.

INFORMATION ABOUT RELATED TOPICS

Tim Brooks and Earle Marsh, *The Complete Directory to Prime Time Network TV Shows, 1946–Present.* New York: Ballantine Books, 1979.

Paddy Chayefsky, *Television Plays.* New York: Simon & Schuster, 1955.

Shari S. Diamond and Hans Zeisel, "Jury Behavior," in Sanford H. Kadish, *Encyclopedia of Crime and Justice.* New York: Free Press, 1983.

James F. Gilsinan, *Doing Justice: How the System Works—as Seen by the Participants.* Englewood Cliffs, NJ: Prentice-Hall, 1982.

Walter Goodman, *The Committee: The Extraordinary Career of the House Committee on Un-American Activities.* New York: Farrar, Straus, and Giroux, 1968.

Allen J. Hart, "Jury Psychology," in V.S. Ramachandran, *Encyclopedia of Human Behavior.* San Diego: Academic Press, 1994.

William Hawes, *American Television Drama: The Experimental Years.* Tuscaloosa: University of Alabama Press, 1986.

R.D. Heldenfels, *Television's Greatest Year: 1954.* New York: Continuum, 1994.

Ronald L. Jacobson, ed., *Television Research: A Directory of Conceptual Categories, Topic Suggestions, and Selected Sources.* Jefferson, NC, and London: McFarland, 1995.

Pauline Kael, *I Lost It at the Movies.* Boston: Atlantic Monthly Press, 1965.

J. Fred MacDonald, *One Nation Under Television: The Rise and Fall of Network TV.* New York: Pantheon Books, 1990.

Joseph R. McCarthy, *McCarthyism: The Fight for America.* New York: Arno Press, 1977.

Peter Roffman and Jim Purdy, *The Hollywood Social Problem Film: Madness, Despair, and Politics from the Depression to the Fifties.* Bloomington: Indiana University Press, 1981.

Howard Rosenberg, "Fifties TV: Gold or Dross?" *American Film,* December 1981.

Thomas Ross, *Just Stories: How the Law Embodies Racism and Bias.* Boston: Beacon Press, 1966.

Tom Stempel, *Storytellers to the Nation: A History of American Television Writing.* New York: Continuum, 1992.

Max Wilk, *The Golden Age of Television.* New York: Delacorte Press, 1976.

Melvyn Bernard Zerman, *Beyond a Reasonable Doubt: Inside the American Jury System.* New York: Thomas Y. Crowell, 1981.

INDEX